812

C000177783

avoi -

I hope this
deepens your
understanding.
with love
and appreciation.

C
2015

I

DEDICATE THIS BOOK

TO

URSULA M. NIEBUHR

THE WIFE AND COMRADE OF THE

SUBJECT OF THE BOOK

PREFACE

To write a book on a contemporary thinker, especially a thinker of such eminence as Reinhold Niebuhr, has in it an element of presumption. When all is said, nobody can interpret Niebuhr so well as Niebuhr himself. There is the man, a living influence in two continents. His books are easily available for all who care to read. They are written in vigorous, clear, simple American English which anyone of average intelligence can grasp. Why then write a book about a man which, at best, will be inferior to the books of the man himself? A very reasonable question, and very much to the point. The following pages can only be justified by a satisfactory answer to that question.

First, then, in a series of books about contemporary Christian revolutionaries,[1] if such a series is to be remotely representative, the omission of Reinhold Niebuhr is impossible. That in itself constitutes a sufficiently good reason for writing on Niebuhr. A series purporting to describe and discuss living Christian revolutionaries which omitted Niebuhr would be ridiculous. Comparisons are invidious, but this at least may

[1] The present book on Reinhold Niebuhr is part of the Modern Christian Revolutionaries series, edited by Donald Attwater. Five other books of this series have been brought out in a single volume, *Modern Christian Revolutionaries,* published by the Devin-Adair Company.

be said: that among the Christian revolutionaries of
both Europe and America today, there is, most certainly, none greater, more significant or more influential
than Reinhold Niebuhr. A series which by-passed him
would be self-condemned. "Where MacTavish sits is
the head of the table." Niebuhr is one of the most vital
centres of Christian thinking in politics and sociology
today.

But there is another and even stronger reason for this
book. The present writer has been deeply impressed,
and very much surprised at first, by the frequency with
which well-educated and intelligent people have confessed that they do not understand Dr. Niebuhr, that
they "can't get the hang" of what he is saying. In lecturing to students and clergy and ministers of all denominations, the present writer has come across scores
of men (among whom Oxford and Cambridge were
well represented) who failed to grasp Dr. Niebuhr's
position. They confessed to being confused by what
they could not help thinking was Dr. Niebuhr's inconsistencies and self-contradictions. As one—quite intelligent—person put it: "Niebuhr no sooner makes a statement than he seems to affirm the opposite." In other
words, there are a number of people who, in spite of their
eagerness to read and understand Niebuhr, fail to understand what he is saying, because of their unfamili-
arity with *his way of thinking*. Reinhold Niebuhr is a
supremely "dialectical" thinker. In his mental process, "either . . . or" is balanced by "both . . . and."
Readers who can only think in terms of "either . . .
or" therefore find him difficult, and so are missing

one of the most vital and profound contributions to contemporary Christian thought. This fact seems to indicate the need for a book of the kind attempted here.

But in many cases the failure to understand Dr. Niebuhr is due, in the final analysis, not to inadequate intellectual processes, but to a defective attitude to life, and more especially to religion. This attitude may be described as an insufficient appreciation of the tragic element in moral experience, and of the abysmal element in religion, particularly in Christianity. Men to whom life is essentially simple and capable of a purely rational comprehension will always find it difficult to understand men who are burdened by the realization of the ultimate inscrutability and incalculability of life and religion. To this latter class belongs Dr. Niebuhr. His awareness of the depth beneath the depths makes it impossible for him to comprehend man's tragic history in a neat formula, without torn and ragged edges. In the contradictory being of man there is an ultimate abyss which defies smooth, rational statement. Dr. Niebuhr is unusual and exceptional in this : reared in a civilization of optimism, which manifested the maximum of human power over environment, he nevertheless was impressed more by man's tragic weakness than by his dazzling achievements. In this he is a very untypical American, but very typical of prophetic Christianity. In his sociological thinking he has anticipated a whole social development. He has kept one step ahead of history. That's what makes him a prophetic, Christian revolutionary. But also it is what makes him diffi-

cult for so many good, uncomplicated souls to understand.

I have undertaken the task of endeavoring to interpret Dr. Niebuhr to English readers with some diffidence, yet also with some relish. With diffidence, because one is anxious to do justice to a great contemporary figure in Christian theology and sociology. But I
am emboldened to essay this task by the knowledge that
my own theological and political development has been
somewhat similar to Dr. Niebuhr's. In his generous—
too generous—review of my first book, *On To Orthodoxy* (*vide British Weekly,* September 14, 1939), Dr.
Niebuhr wrote that his own experience had been similar
to mine. This means that I approach Dr. Niebuhr's
thinking from the inside, from an inner comprehension
which considerably illuminates the study of his writing.

I have accepted the invitation to write this book with
relish for the simple reason that it gives me the opportunity to express publicly my great indebtedness to Dr.
Niebuhr. I first came across his work during a deep
crisis in my own inner life, which Dr. Niebuhr, more
than any contemporary thinker, helped me to resolve.
If I can mediate him to men and women who may be
struggling in the throes of some similar crisis, I shall
feel amply justified and rewarded.

I must not conclude this already too lengthy preface
without expressing my warmest thanks to Dr. Niebuhr
for his willingness to supply me with information. I
have the liveliest and happiest recollections of a whole
precious day which he gave to me in the midst of a
crowded visit he made to England in 1943. His gen-

erous friendship, no less than his profound and acute writings, inspire in me the deepest gratitude. Needless to say, he bears no responsibility for this book which is entirely mine.

My grateful thanks are also due to Dr. Niebuhr's English publishers, Messrs. James Nisbet & Co., Ltd., for kind permission to make quotations from his Gifford lectures, *The Nature and Destiny of Man,* and *Beyond Tragedy.*

D. R. DAVIES

BOOKS BY REINHOLD NIEBUHR

The reader is advised to begin his study of Niebuhr with a little work which will give him some feeling of Niebuhr the man, *Leaves from the Notebook of a Tamed Cynic*. Here the reader will see Niebuhr struggling to adapt himself to the demands and duties of a parish ministry. It is the struggle of an intensely human being, who will thus commend himself to the reader. The best introduction to Niebuhr's work is, I think, the book *Does Modern Civilization Need Religion?* in which are formulated most of his characteristic ideas, which he presents in more developed form in later work. The specific problem of the relevance of Christianity to civilization is best studied, to begin with at least, in *An Interpretation of Christian Ethics*. Niebuhr formulates the question here in more systematic form. His critique of contemporary civilization can be read in *Moral Man and Immoral Society* and in *Reflections on the End of an Era*. The above volumes should be thoroughly read and mastered before proceeding to the two volumes of Gifford lectures, but the reader should make certain of reading them in the end, for these two volumes, *The Nature and Destiny of Man*, are indispensable, books to be bought and not just borrowed.

Does Modern Civilization Need Religion? Macmillan, 1928.
Leaves from the Notebook of a Tamed Cynic. Harper, 1930.
The Contribution of Religion to Social Work. (Forbes Lectures.) Columbia University Press, 1932.
Moral Man and Immoral Society. Scribner, 1933.
Reflections on the End of an Era. Scribner, 1934.
An Interpretation of Christian Ethics. (Rauchenbusch Memorial Lectures.) Harper, 1935.
Does the State and Nation Belong to God or the Devil? (Burge Memorial Lecture.) S.C.M. Press, 1937.
The Protestant Opposition Movement in Germany, 1934–37. Friends of Europe, 1937.
Beyond Tragedy: Essays on the Christian Interpretation of History. Nisbet, 1938; Scribner.
Why the Christian Church Is Not Pacifist. S.C.M. Press, 1940; Macmillan, Toronto.

Europe's Catastrophe and the Christian Faith. Nisbet, 1940.

Christianity and Power Politics. Scribner, 1940; Nisbet.

The Nature and Destiny of Man. (Gifford Lectures.) 2 vols. Nisbet, 1941–3; Scribner.

Jews After the War. University Jewish Federation of Great Britain, 1943.

The Children of Darkness and the Children of Light. Scribner, 1944; Nisbet.

CONTENTS

1

The Making of a Revolutionary

REINHOLD NIEBUHR, as his name suggests, is of German extraction, though he is a full American citizen. His American birth and rearing, together with his German origin, may partly account for the unusual combination in him of qualities which nearly always are separate; for Niebuhr is distinguished by the fact of an intense awareness of ultimate problems allied with an equally intense preoccupation with the immediate, concrete, practical next step. In most men these qualities exist in isolation from each other. As a rule, men who are absorbed in the contemplation of the final, ultimate problems of human existence are oblivious to the relative, practical necessities under which men have to live. They do not feel the pressure and the urgency of the concrete political and social problems demanding some kind of solution or other. The theologian or philosopher, wrestling with the great problems of the nature of being, the destiny of man, the purpose and meaning of existence, usually has no mind for the immediate political problem. And vice-versa, the man who finds the breath of life in tackling the emerging problems of contemporary social and historic development hardly ever lifts his mind to the level of final issues. Niebuhr

1

is one of those rare thinkers in whose mind these two phases—the immediate and the ultimate—are in an organic, dynamic relation. They are not static entities in his mind. It is not that he has a spell, so to speak, during which his mind is given over to immediate issues —the new form of international relationships, the next step in social legislation, etc.; then another spell during which his mind becomes absorbed with questions of eschatology, the significance of Providence in history, etc. Niebuhr's thinking is a process in which every immediate problem is set in the context of the ultimate, and the ultimate reality is informed with concrete historic content by its relation to immediate social issues. His thinking faithfully reflects the tension of daily experience.

This combination may be partly due, as already suggested, to Niebuhr's German origin and to his American birth and environment. In his veins there mingle the blood of the German philosopher and that of the "Anglo-Saxon" politician and practician. The German mind functions naturally and at its best—it is its genius—in the contemplation of the ultimate mysteries of thought. Characteristic of the German mind is the Hegelian attempt to systematize the Absolute, and the Kantian attempt to formulate the nature of knowing, to relate practical reason and pure reason. The raw material of German philosophy is the final mystery of *being*. But English philosophy, from which the chief element of the American mind derives, is concerned mainly with practical political problems—Hobbes and what constitutes the state; Locke and what constitutes society.

Hume, it is true, goes beyond these questions—but Hume was a Scotsman. Americanism is a "stepping-stone" of "Anglo-Saxon" mentality. It is in the nature of things that pluralism should be an American philosophical product, in which the Absolute is reduced to a mere succession of relativities. American civilization had, of course, to deal with an immediate practical problem, which brooked no delay. Thus the American mind, which has been shaped by the demands of the immediate, is the antithesis of the German mind. But in Reinhold Niebuhr, the German mentality and temper, with a zest for the immediate job to be done—these twain have been fused into a new mentality, in which the concrete and the ultimate hold on to each other in a restless tension.

He was born on June 21, 1892, the son of a German Evangelical pastor, Gustav Niebuhr, so that he is a son of the manse. And here it may be well to kill the legend, so widespread in Great Britain, that he was reluctant to enter the ministry. It is simply not true. He was brought up in a pastor's home and he remembers, with gratitude, his father's prayers at the family altar. His father, who was a keen theological student, of liberal tendencies, and a deeply cultured man, did not bring any pressure to bear on Niebuhr to enter the ministry. But he relates that, after considerable thought, he decided, on his own initiative, to become a minister. It was with great rejoicing that his father heard the news, to whom he communicated it in the simple words, "Father, I want to become a minister." There can be no doubt whatever that Niebuhr felt quite certain of his vocation. He felt no reluctance of any kind about becoming a minister. He did feel some doubt whether he should exercise his ministry in the German Evangelical Church, which was one of the smaller, lesser-known and narrower off-shoots of the German Lutheran Church. Niebuhr probably felt the urge to swim in the broader, fuller stream of American religious life, compared to which the German Evangelical Church of the early nineteen-hundreds was a sluggish backwater. But Neibuhr's hesitation was not whether to become a minister or not, but whether to become a German Evangelical minister, and whether to become a parish minister or a theological teacher. One of Niebuhr's professors, Macintosh, influenced him in the direction of theological teaching. On completion of his course at Elmhurst College (the denominational school) and Yale University, Niebuhr was "ordered," in accordance with the practice of the body, to take up the parochial ministry of Bethel Evangelical church in Detroit. With his mind set on teaching, perhaps there was some reluctance to enter on the work of a parish; for Niebuhr confesses that he "entered and left the parish ministry against my inclinations . . ." [1]

As a matter of fact, however, Niebuhr did not quite complete the educational course he had originally in-

---

[1] Vide *Leaves from the Notebook of a Tamed Cynic,* p. xii. This is a book of priceless wisdom for theological students. It consists of extracts from a diary which Dr. Niebuhr kept during his thirteen years' pastorate. An English edition would be a great boon to students. It would probably save them from many of the errors and pitfalls in which the Christian ministry of all denominations so amply abounds.

tended. After reading arts and a certain amount of theology at Elmhurst College, he went to Yale with the idea of reading for a doctorate in theology, for this was the necessary passport to a professorship in theology. But before attaining the degree Niebuhr—as he himself puts it—"quit." By the time he graduated as master of arts, for which he read a considerable amount of theology, he had become irritated by the irrelevance of much of his theological study to the actual daily life around him. I do not mean by this what so many theological students mean when they revolt against scientific discipline. Many men who merely dislike the study, *e.g.,* of Biblical languages, church history, systematic doctrine, etc., rationalize their reluctance to submit to intellectual discipline by persuading themselves that all this has nothing to do with the actual work of the ministry. Their feeling of irrelevance is a convenient camouflage for laziness. This was not what Niebuhr felt; for, quite obviously, the pursuit of ideas is a natural passion with him, an activity delightful for its own sake. What he felt was something very different, and was the first symptom of his possession by a Christian revolutionary spirit.

In the years of Niebuhr's theological training, religious liberalism [2] was at its height, especially in Amer-

---

[2] What term should one use to describe the theological tendency which was dominated by modern rationalism and the idea of inevitable progress? "Humanism" is hardly correct, since it lacks the religious element: it was a secular philosophy of man and history. "Modernism" is misleading, since it conveys the impression that modern advances in knowledge and science are objected to by its opponents—which, of course, is not the case. So in these pages, I

ica, where it was the natural and almost inevitable consequence in theology of the gigantic conquests of American skill and technique. Orthodoxy was at a discount. For a theological student in the early nineteen-hundreds to be orthodox was an anachronism. To be in the swim one had to be liberal. The bright young men inevitably found their way onto the band-wagon of liberalism. "I believe in the forgiveness of sins, the resurrection of the body and the life everlasting." Of these words Niebuhr writes:

"These closing words of the Apostolic creed, in which the Christian hope of the fulfilment of life is expressed, were, as I remember it, an offence and a stumbling-block to young theologians at the time when my generation graduated from theological seminaries. Those of us who were expected to express our Christian faith in terms of the Apostolic creed at the occasion of our ordination had long and searching discussions on the problem presented by the creed, particularly by the last phrase. We were not certain that we could honestly express our faith in such a formula. If we were finally prevailed upon to do so, it was usually with a patronizing air toward the Christian past, with which we desired to express a sense of unity even if the price was the suppression of our moral and theological scruples over its inadequate rendering of the Christian faith. The

shall stick to the terms "religious liberalism," or "Protestant liberalism," for the Roman Catholic Church never dallied with the liberal movement in theology.

twenty years which divide that time from this have brought great changes in theological thought though I am not certain that many of my contemporaries are not still of the same mind in which they were then. Yet some of us have been persuaded to take the stone which we then rejected and make it the head of the corner. In other words, there is no part of the Apostolic creed which, in our present opinion, expresses the whole genius of the Christian faith more nearly than just this despised phrase: 'I believe in the resurrection of the body!' " (*Beyond Tragedy,* pp. 289–90. Charles Scribner's Sons.)

This passage expresses well the theological temper of the time in which Niebuhr was preparing for the ministry. It is significant that his reaction to it should be, in the first instance, not intellectual, but moral and psychological. Already Niebuhr was beginning to feel faintly that the predominating theological liberalism of his time was not relevant to the concrete problems of life and daily experience. It did not fit into the context of the conflicting issues of the American scene. This easy, optimistic gospel of roaring, irresistible movement to Utopia was already beginning to sound out of tune somehow in the youthful student's ears.

Now this is a most remarkable, significant fact, the importance of which the reader might easily miss. In reacting in this way to the theological liberalism of his time, Niebuhr was anticipating an entire process of historic development. In the triumphant peak of social progress, when the actual situation was so gloriously

confirming faith in collective omnipotence, when, as yet,
it conveyed no hint of the wrath to come, Niebuhr's
ears caught the muffled echoes of the distant—very distant—thunder. With most Christian thinkers the situation is quite the reverse. They only become aware of
social tendencies as they are passing away. They follow
historic development a long way behind. They recognize and condemn social evils only when even the blind
can no longer ignore them. There is nothing particularly prophetic in such an attitude. But Niebuhr was
beginning to sense the coming storm and crisis of civilization when the sky was still apparently cloudless. It
was this "sixth-sense" of his which was the source of
his feeling that so much of the theology he was imbibing
in his college days was irrelevant. His revolutionary
spirit, therefore, was native to him, fundamental and
inherent in his make-up, in his very being. It is necessary to emphasize this point. He did not acquire it as
the result of a rational process by the study of some
analytical sociology, such as Marxism. At this time,
1910–1915, he had not yet read Marx nor made contact with general Marxist literature. All this was to
come later. His sensing of the underlying tragic and
corrupting element in the social situation was the sign
of his own creative, prophetic mind. One cannot
"explain" this, in the sense of enumerating and
analyzing all the factors that caused or determined it.
One can but recognize it as something already in
operation.

So with this irritating consciousness of the irrelevance of much that he was perforce being compelled to
learn, Niebuhr did not proceed to his doctor's degree,

which meant that he could not undertake a professorship. It, therefore, had to be the parochial cure of souls.

In the German Evangelical Church individual con-
gregations did not invite men; the practice was for the
central authority to place men in churches, a practice
for which, in retrospect, Niebuhr feels there is a great
deal to be said. So on leaving Yale after graduating
M.A., Niebuhr was sent to undertake the pastorate of
Bethel Evangelical church in Detroit in 1915. At that
time it was but a small community of only eighteen
families. As subsequent events showed, it was a good
sphere in which to begin. The pastoral side of his ministry did not make too great a tax on his intellectual and
spiritual resources, though he certainly felt the strain,
both intellectually and spiritually. For instance, after he
had preached about a dozen times, Niebuhr felt he had
said all he had to say. "Now that I have preached about
a dozen sermons, I find I am repeating myself. A different text simply means a different pretext for saying
the same thing over again. The few ideas that I had
worked into sermons at the seminary have all been
used, and now what?" (*Leaves from the Notebook
of a Tamed Cynic,* p. 4. Harper & Brothers.)

Thus Niebuhr felt acutely the need to read and
study. His desire was painfully accentuated by the
necessities of his ministry. He was greatly handicapped
by his inability to buy books: during the first five
years of his pastorate he bought hardly a single one.
His very small salary made it impossible. It was during
these years that he was so greatly preoccupied by the
intellectual aspect of theology, and so needed most to
get books. Later on, as the result of his pastoral work

among the workers in the Ford plant, and of his own social observation, the ethical aspect of theological problems overshadowed the purely rational aspect in his thinking. We find this entry in his diary in 1920 after five years in the pastorate. "I am beginning to like the ministry. I think since I have stopped worrying so much about the intellectual problems of religion and have begun to explore some of its ethical problems there is more of a thrill in preaching. The real meaning of the gospel is in conflict with most of the customs and attitudes of our day at so many places that there is adventure in the Christian message, even if you only play around with its ideas in a conventional world" (*op. cit.*, p. 27).

Another instance of the strain which Niebuhr felt in these first five years arose from his acute personal shyness and sensitiveness, which, however, contributed greatly to his revolutionary development. It seems to be a law, both in personal experience and in the wider social development of civilization, that it is through the overcoming of what is painful and difficult that the best insights and achievements are realized. Dr. Niebuhr demonstrates this within the more restricted range of the experience of the individual. He found pastoral visitation, at first, to be most painful and difficult. To visit people in their homes and talk to them in terms of personal intimacy, which the pastoral office necessitates if it is to be genuinely exercised, he felt was something of an agony. He writes, "I am glad there are only eighteen families in this church. I have been visiting the members for six weeks, and haven't seen all of them

yet. Usually I walk past a house two or three times before I summon the courage to go in. I am always very
courteously received, so I don't know exactly why I
should not be able to overcome this curious timidity"
(*op. cit.,* p. 3). It was precisely through his subsequent
personal contacts with Ford workers and others that
Niebuhr came to comprehend the profoundly tragic and
contradictory character of human nature as manifested
in social and economic relationships. In his first essays
at personal contacts with the members of his congregation he was laying the foundations of his profound and
sincere personal interest and concern with the exploited
classes of capitalist society. It is in this awareness of
the reality of the personal that Niebuhr so finely dis-
plays the Christian revolutionary spirit. The defeat and
tragedy of the secular revolutionary is that the reality
of the individual as a person, an end in himself, is dissipated into mere social forces and institutionalism. The
individual as a soul, a person, degenerates into a factor
in the class or social struggle, especially in the crisis of
an actual revolutionary situation. That is one reason
why, in due course, the revolutionary can, in his turn,
oppress and exploit the very people he set out to emanci-
pate. This tendency to instrumentalize living souls, to
which both secular and Christian revolutionaries are
subject, was held in check in Niebuhr's case by the cost-
liness with which he had learnt to secure personal contacts and intimacy in the course of his pastoral work.
A reality acquired under so much stress offered a tough
resistance to the corrupting processes of institutionalism.

The fact that Niebuhr increasingly tended to en-
visage and formulate theological problems in the frame-
work of concrete personal relationships helps, perhaps,
to explain a rare quality in Niebuhr—a quality, more-
over, which constituted an important element in his
make-up as a Christian revolutionary. This quality was
an acute and constant awareness of the corrupting
element in his own profession of Christian minister,
and in his own ideas and interests. This capacity to see
in oneself the tendency to self-deception and humbug-
ging is rare in any and every calling, in the Christian
ministry as in other professions: indeed, one may say
especially in the Christian ministry. This power of
"self-criticism," which later, in the Russian Communist party, was to become a cant phrase, was to become
one of the major themes in Niebuhr's social analysis,
and the one on which he has written with most power
and illumination. We find almost at the beginning of
his ministry that he was becoming aware of how fatally
the will-to-power and egoistic compensation and satisfaction insinuated themselves into the most exalted
activities of the ministerial office.

"Beside the brutal facts of modern industrial life,
how futile are all our homiletical spoutings! The
Church is undoubtedly cultivating graces and preserving spiritual amenities in the more protected areas of our
society. But it isn't changing the essential facts of modern industrial civilization by a hair's breadth" (op. cit.,
p. 79). Here is an instance of Niebuhr's refusal to
close his eyes to fundamental facts. In the next quota-
tion he indicates the general clerical reaction to this
situation—a reaction in which he sees his own partici-

pation. He places himself on the same level as those whom he blames. That is, he criticizes, but does not judge. "But I must confess that I haven't discovered much courage in the ministry. The average parson is characterized by suavity and circumspection rather than by robust fortitude. I do not intend to be mean in my criticism, because I am a coward myself and find it tremendously difficult to run counter to general opinion" (*op. cit.*, p. 110). But he goes deeper than this.

"One of the most fruitful sources of self-deception in the ministry is the proclamation of great ideals and principles without any clue to their relation to the controversial issues of the day. The minister feels very heroic in uttering the ideals because he knows that some rather dangerous immediate consequences are involved in their application. But he doesn't make the application clear, and those who hear his words are either unable to see the immediate issue involved or they are unconsciously grateful to the preacher for not belaboring a contemporaneous issue which they know to be involved but would rather not face. I have myself too frequently avoided the specific application of general principles to controversial situations to be able to deny what really goes on in the mind of the preacher when he is doing this. I don't think I have always avoided it, and when I haven't I have invariably gotten into some difficulty" (*op. cit.*, pp. 191–2).

This passage illustrates, as does the whole book from which it is quoted, how close Niebuhr keeps to concrete, actual experience. And here, I think, is the explanation of one of the great qualities of Niebuhr, namely, his relevance to the whole contemporary situation of man in history. One of his greatest achievements is that he has made theology a science of secular urgency and significance. He is one of the very few theologians to whom secular and humanist thinkers pay attention, as much as they pay to their own publicists. This is a most rare achievement, of which few theologians can boast. In England, we can count them on the fingers of one hand, of whom one would undoubtedly be Mr. C. S. Lewis. Theology in the hands of the typical theologians of all schools has somehow come to seem remote from current issues and problems, an abstract, slightly faddist, pursuit. But, as Niebuhr presents it, it becomes a living, contemporary issue, more up-to-date than *The Times,* and certainly less pompous. Most men write *about* theology. But Niebuhr writes theology straight from the furnace of social conflict and tragedy. Theology, to Niebuhr, is no "ivory castle." It is thus because in his pastorate, his one and only pastorate, he was all the time under the pressure of hard, material realities; for—an important factor—he lived for thirteen years in Detroit.

* * *

One of the greatest influences that went to the making of a Christian revolutionary out of Niebuhr was—Henry Ford. Needless to say, Mr. Ford did not intend that, and, in all probability, was blissfully unaware that he had done any such thing. But this is in the fitness of Providence, which has always displayed a profound

ironical sense of humor. Out of man's productive activity, Providence manufactures a by-product. St. Paul,
the missionary, was one of the providential by-products
of the Roman Empire. And Reinhold Niebuhr, the
Christian revolutionary, was one of the by-products
of Mr. Henry Ford's motor manufacture. At the same
time as he was producing his tin-lizzies (which at a
later stage he made into ladies) Mr. Ford was also
producing at least one Christian revolutionary. Probably many more. But we are sure that he produced one.

In 1915, the year in which Niebuhr began his work
in the ministry, his church had little more than forty
members. In 1928, when he became professor of applied Christian ethics at Union Seminary, New York,
he left behind him a flourishing church of over 800
members. Niebuhr himself is very modest about this
magnificent achievement. He says that any person,
short of an utter incompetent, could have built a church
in those hectic years, during which the population of
Detroit increased from a hundred thousand to nearly
a million. Whilst we shall thoroughly disagree with
Niebuhr's own estimate of himself as a church-builder,
we must acknowledge that the great increase in Detroit's population was a most favorable factor. It gave
Niebuhr the opportunity, which he so splendidly turned
to account.

The dominant factor in this great growth of population was, of course, the great expansion in the Ford
industries. After Henry Ford's romantic attempt with
the ridiculous "peace ship" to end European hostilities
in the war of 1914–18, and when America entered the

war in 1917, Ford settled down to organize gigantic
production for the American and associated armies.
This meant a greatly extended plant and a vast increase
in labor-power. This was the source of the increase of
Detroit's population, which had to be catered for re-
ligiously as well as secularly. Niebuhr attracted both
young and old to his church, and to some extent the
age distinction coincided with the political complexion
of his congregation. The younger people in the congregation tended to be "radical," in the American sense
of the word, *i.e.*, left-wing, progressive and liberal. The
older people tended to be more conservative. Thus Niebuhr's congregation was nicely balanced, which partly
accounts for the comparatively little trouble which he
experienced as a result of his preaching and teaching.
Niebuhr not only enunciated principles to which, as he
says, nobody objects, he also indicated applications of
those principles to current social issues, to which many
people object. Niebuhr of course did not escape altogether. How could he? But the presence in his congregation of numerous radical-thinking young people kept
the trouble within bounds.

It was through his contact with the Ford workers,
both inside his church and outside, that Niebuhr's attitude to social problems took shape; for he had opportunity to observe in the lives of people the inhuman
effects of Ford's spurious idealism. And it taught him
one thing in particular: the penetration of idealism by
the corrupting element of self-interest; the inevitability
of self-deception in the best intentions; the underlying
cruelty and brutality in every class culture. He learnt

this as a fact of living, sensitive, human suffering. On the one hand were the loudly-trumpeted Ford principles of industrial organization in capitalist press and speeches throughout the world. On the other hand Niebuhr saw the results of those same principles at work in the daily life of men, women and children. So he learnt that social idealism could never be taken at face-value. He learnt that, not as an abstract principle, but as a pathological human process, as something that made men anxious and women fearful. There was in Niebuhr's social observation a profound prophetic quality, by means of which he was enabled to feel the struggle and suffering of people as a personal thing. He combined with the exactitude, the fact-finding mind of the social scientist, the passionate spirit and the religious insight of the prophet. Which serves to describe the Christian revolutionary, who is a synthesis of social scientist and religious prophet, of historic realism and super-historic revelation. It may be useful to give a few instances of Niebuhr's reactions to the Ford environment in Detroit.

At the close of the last war, from 1920 till about 1928, America experienced a phase of material progress and prosperity. Every class in society enjoyed a relatively high standard of living. Money was abundant, and commodities hitherto regarded as luxuries of the privileged few entered into common use. Radios, automobiles and refrigerators became a general possession. To be without these was a sign of poverty. People of small incomes were enabled to negotiate the high prices of these and similar commodities by a fantastic development of the hire-purchase system. At one bound, America had entered into Eldorado. Was it not the land in which every working-man went to his work in his own motor car? It is difficult in our present situation to recapture the atmosphere of untroubled optimism and irresponsible confidence that prevailed in that cloud-cuckoo land which America was in that boom period. At long last, the problem of poverty had been solved. The apologists for American capitalism laughed at the jeremiads of Marx and all the other prophets of gloom. Capitalism was functioning beautifully. At one and the same time it milled out extravagant profits to the capitalist at one end, and abundant wages to the proletariat at the other. High wages became a capitalist argument. The solemn economic experts were taken in. The Marxist analysis of surplus value was jeered at. "The fundamental business of the country," said President Hoover, "is on a sound and prosperous basis."

Now the leader of the hosts which had planted the New Jerusalem in America's vast and varied land was Henry Ford, to whom "history is bunk." He claimed specifically three things: that he served the public by providing it with a good, cheap car; that he paid his workers high wages, a minimum of five dollars a day; that he secured them an ample leisure by instituting the five-day week. The world gaped in admiration at the Ford miracle. Reinhold Niebuhr, being on the spot and being in personal touch with the men for whom these wonderful things were being done, reacted differently.

Mr. Seebohm Rowntree, after a visit which he paid to the Ford works, said that it was the nearest thing to hell he had ever seen. That was the aspect of it which impinged on Niebuhr. All this triumph of organization, with its efficient service and its alleged benefits to the worker, was a vast mechanism which dehumanized and depersonalized the worker at the same time. It was all built up on the principle of a scientific reduction of physical movement to a minimum and of adapting the worker, the human agent, to the remorseless continuity of the machine. It was the worker, enslaved by the conveyor belt, who paid the price for this in nervous tension. Not Ford himself; nor the new technicians of labor-processes with their soulless research into the behavior of human beings in the factory; nor the public, who little realized that the gallivanting jaunts which their tin-lizzie made possible were the result of the torn nerves of living men. Material progress might demand too great a price in human consciousness. "We went through one of the big automobile factories to-day. . . . The foundry interested me particularly. The heat was terrific. The men seemed weary. Here manual labor is a drudgery and toil is slavery. The men cannot possibly find any satisfaction in their work. They simply work to make a living. Their sweat and their dull pain are part of the price paid for the fine cars we all run. And most of us run the cars without knowing what price is being paid for them. . . . We are all responsible. We all want the things which the factory produces and none of us is sensitive enough to care how much in human values the efficiency of the modern factory costs" (*op. cit.,* pp. 79–80). "The culture of every society seeks to obscure the brutalities on which

it rests." In Niebuhr's vision the brutalities loomed
larger than the loudly trumpeted progress and achievements. This vision made of him a permanent, penetrating critic of the entire social structure. He would con-
cede the first of Ford's claims, namely that he provided
the public with a good, cheap car. But over against that
fact, Niebuhr was oppressed by the human misery it
cost.

Ford's second claim, that he paid high wages to his
workers, especially that the minimum was five dollars
a day, probably did as much as anything to push Niebuhr in a revolutionary direction. Factually and liter-
ally, of course, the claim could not be challenged. Even
the floor-sweeper did get his five dollars *for every day
that he worked*. But the implications were specious and
misleading. The general assumption was that five dollars a day meant thirty dollars a week, fifteen hundred
dollars a year of fifty weeks. The doorkeepers in Ford's
factories were in receipt of the sumptuous salary of
£300 a year. That was the general belief. But it didn't
work out that way. Not by a long chalk. Hardly a single
one of Ford's vast army of workers ever managed to
work six days a week, fifty weeks a year. The reality,
therefore, behind the splendid façade of "five dollars
a day" was for great numbers a squalid poverty, which
at times and for certain periods was grim and acute.
The five dollars per day, by the end of the year,
amounted to far less than fifteen hundred. I cannot
pretend to give exact figures. But of the general fact,
there could be no doubt: that owing to the number of
days in the course of a year that they did not work,

masses of Ford's workers in Detroit struggled along in acute poverty.

"What a civilization this is! Naïve gentlemen with a genius for mechanics suddenly become the arbiters over the lives and fortunes of hundreds and thousands. Their moral pretensions are credulously accepted at full value. No one bothers to ask whether an industry which can maintain a cash reserve of a quarter of a billion ought not make some provision for its unemployed. . . . The cry of the hungry is drowned in the song, 'Henry has made a lady out of Lizzy' " (*op. cit.*, pp. 154–5).

The third of Mr. Ford's claims was the most pretentious of all. Again, in the bare literal sense, it is quite true that in the course of a week his factory worked less hours for the same pay—but at a much greater cost. He instituted the five-day week on the iniquitous speed-up principle. And if I may use a colloquialism, this is what got Niebuhr's goat. Ford's labor engineers worked out a greater speed-up and concentration of physical processes in the factory, by means of which the workers were compelled to effect a *greater production in five days than in the previous six*. So the Ford works switched over to five days a week, as a result of which there was a slight increase in production, and a slight decrease in financial cost, but a greater expenditure of nervous energy and nervous wear and tear. The cheapening of the economic cost of production of the Ford car resulted inevitably in the cheapening also of the personality of the producer.

Every one of Ford's supposed benefits for the workers was of still greater benefit to Henry Ford—which rather takes the gilt off the gingerbread. In every case, it was the public that stumped up the cash, and the workers themselves who paid in additional nervous wear and tear. It was "enlightened self-interest" with a vengeance.

Thus the thirteen years Niebuhr lived in Detroit were spent in seeing the moral and social consequences and implications of brutal economic facts. It was a discipline which made him a revolutionary; for he revolted against it with his whole soul. It made of him a Christian revolutionary, since his revolt was determined by the vision of man as free personality, as one meant to be son of God. It is significant and fitting that this should have happened in Detroit. Henry Ford was the personal symbol of machine-power, mass-production, etc., his vision was one of "machines to make more machines." Reinhold Niebuhr was a symbol too, a symbol of the response of the Christian gospel to this latest and greatest peril to the soul of man.

* * *

During these thirteen years of intense activity in Detroit, Niebuhr became known nationally as a thorough-going "radical"—a term which connoted everything opprobrious. In no country did the bolshevik bogey exercise a more searing influence among the middle classes than in the United States throughout the immediate post-war years. The country was swept by an unreasoning torrent of panic, when socialists, communists and liberals (lumped together as "radicals"), were savagely persecuted. It was, therefore, a very difficult and dangerous time in which to evince social sympathies. It speaks volumes for the personality and character of Niebuhr that, through all this panic, his influence continued to grow. He did not trim his revolutionary sails to the winds of reaction.

As well as being in daily personal and pastoral contact with the members of his congregation, Niebuhr was also closely associated with labor and socialist organizations outside his church, a fact which constituted an excellent dialectical discipline. In this way he was compelled to relate his Christianity to a concrete human situation, and to relate social problems to Christian theology. This as much as anything was what molded him into a Christian revolutionary, since his relation to non-church socialist groups made him familiar with non-Christian revolutionary ideas and literature. The artificiality and secular ignorance of so many men in the ministry of all denominations is due to their restriction to professional church life. Their whole life almost is spent among church circles. Their reading is confined to professional theology, with the result that their knowledge of the world is refracted through a prism of religiosity. This breeds a certain pious unreality. Religious authorities might do worse than to make it compulsory for Christian ministers, during the first ten years of their ministry, to belong to some purely secular organizations. This was Niebuhr's practice throughout his entire ministry. His association with outside labor and socialist groups has continued to this day.

It is important to observe that his socialist activities
have not been carried on at the expense of his Christian activities. It happens only too often that Christian
ministers who are active socialists come to be thought
of in the public mind as being socialists first and only
secondly Christian. Their Christianity has become sub-
ordinate to their socialism. The public impression is
that Christianity is definable in terms of socialism.
There can be no doubt that this impression is frequently unjust. But neither can there be any doubt that
it is frequently just. In the minds of many ardent clerical socialists, Christianity is equated to and identified
with socialism. When that happens, then, notwithstand-
ing protestations to the contrary, Christianity does fall
into second place. This has never happened with Reinhold Niebuhr. His Christianity is so obviously primary
and fundamental that even the most prejudiced and
fearful have never thought of him as anything but
Christian.

To what extent his economic and political reading
contributed to his development as a Christian revolutionary one cannot speak with any confidence. That it
informed his mind is, of course, obvious. Nobody can
read Niebuhr without being impressed with the range
and accuracy of his knowledge of economic and political theory and history. But did any of this *make* him
a Christian revolutionary? This raises the question of
what it is which makes men revolutionary or prophetic.
And this is but a variant of the old, old question which
has never yet been satisfactorily answered—What
makes genius? Who can tell? Where or how did Beethoven get his creative power? What was it in Jeremiah

that singled him out for his profound prophetic role? How can we account for the fact that the bourgeois Marx became a revolutionary creator? Or Lenin? If one could answer these questions one might be able to attempt to define the factor which was decisive in making a Christian revolutionary out of Niebuhr. Men are geniuses and prophets in virtue of some mysterious, inner endowment. Genius and prophecy are inexplicable in terms of mere environment. Environment may modify or influence or mold but not *make* a genius or a prophet or a revolutionary in the profound sense. Men are born so or not. The creative pioneer is what he is in virtue of himself. His environment is not decisive for him. For talent, yes; for genius or prophecy, no.

So in all probability the truth about Niebuhr, the Christian revolutionary, is that he was born with a mysterious potentiality, which became conscious through his Detroit experience. His reading and study, whilst of great significance, were really secondary. He read Marx and Engels, for instance, because he already was revolutionary in himself. The distinctive thing about Niebuhr is not his knowledge, though it is great and unusual. What distinguishes him is his profound insight. And that does not come from mere reading or study, else every M.A. or D.D. would be bristling with prophecy. But they are not. Many of them are deadly dull and blind as bats. We cannot do better than accept the fact that Niebuhr is what he is—a Christian revolutionary—and simply note how he has developed and what his activities have been.

*   *   *

In 1928, Niebuhr accepted the invitation to the chair of applied Christian ethics in Union Theological Seminary, New York—which he still occupies with great distinction. It is no exaggeration to say that today he is a world figure, which is fully attested by two facts. First, that he was invited to deliver the Gifford lectures for 1939–40; and second, that Oxford University bestowed on him its degree of doctor of divinity in June, 1943. Only three other Americans have had the honor of being Gifford lecturers, William James, Josiah Royce and John Dewey. And it is well known how jealously Oxford guards its D.D. degree: it bestows it only when it can no longer withhold it—which is an excellent rule for any university in granting its degrees. Niebuhr's Oxford degree is the symbol of his position and influence.

One of his greatest achievements is that he has invested theology with relevance and significance for the contemporary secular mind, a fact which may be illustrated thus. During his visit to England in 1943, he met Kingsley Martin, editor of the *New Statesman and Nation*, and J. B. Priestley. Niebuhr began to talk politics and sociology, but both Mr. Kingsley Martin and Mr. Priestley said that they had wanted to meet him, not to talk politics, but to discuss religion and theology. Mr. Priestley I do not know. But Mr. Kingsley Martin I do know, and I cannot imagine more than two professional theologians whom he would wish to meet for the purpose of discussing religion. Which demonstrates Niebuhr's power to pierce the thickest secular hide. There is no *theologian* to whom the secular "progressives," either here or in America, listen with greater attention than to Reinhold Niebuhr. Such is the position which he has won by long years of activity both as a Christian thinker and as a radical politician.

Since this book is not a study in biography I cannot attempt to tell the story of Niebuhr's activity since he became professor in 1928. It has been prodigious, both in radical politics and in Christian theology. But this brief sketch would be incomplete without some account of his work for the Fellowship of Socialist Christians in America.

It was founded in 1936 by a group of radical Christians, of whom Niebuhr was one, with the object of correlating Christianity and social reconstruction. Its membership is still small and represents but a very tiny minority of American churchmen. But its numbers bear no relation whatever to the value of its work and witness. In its ranks are some of the ablest Christian thinkers of America. Its best work is done by means of its quarterly journal, which was first published under the title *Radical Religion,* later changed to *Christianity and Society,* under which it continues to appear. It cannot be said to flourish financially; such serious journals never do. But it certainly does flourish intellectually. In its pages is to be found the profoundest thinking about the problem of the relations of Christianity to society.

Niebuhr himself edits it, and writes a goodly portion of it quarter by quarter. Its outstanding feature is, in fact, the editorials on current public questions. It is not

too much to say that there is nothing like these contributions of Niebuhr's in contemporary journalism, most
certainly not in contemporary Christian journalism.
With very few exceptions, commentary on public
events in the religious press is but an echo of that in
the secular press. One looks in vain for interpretation
and commentary distinctively Christian. This is what
Niebuhr almost alone does. His editorials are, needless
to say, always well-informed. But more important than
the reliability and fullness of their information is their
profound insight. Niebuhr does two things. First, he
applies Christian theology as a dominating principle of
social criticism, and, second, seeks to indicate the line
of Christian action in any given situation. He thus re-
deems theology from the charge of being remote and
abstract. In his hands, theology is endowed with profound social implications. He supplies it with a razor
edge, which cuts into the pious complacencies of bourgeois religion, and into the equally pious complacencies
and deep-seated illusions of bourgeois politics, both
capitalist and socialist.

Niebuhr is himself an example of the paradox of
Christian faith; for the disturbing feature of the Christian revolutionary is the combination of orthodox
theology with radical politics. Right-wing in religion,
he is left-wing in politics. Niebuhr has helped to kill
the idea that theological orthodoxy is necessarily re-
actionary in social tendency. He has recalled it from a
false and deadly association. Religious orthodoxy has
for long been synonymous with dullness, unadventur-
ousness, "safety" and privilege. Here in England, ortho-

doxy in religion has too often been wedded with Conservatism and a still more reactionary Liberalism. The phrase "high-church toryism" is an indication, and low-church toryism is another indication of the same thing. Socialists among Anglican evangelicals, for example, are very rare. Niebuhr has done much to poleaxe that attitude. Theological orthodoxy has profound revolutionary implications for society. One of the earliest revolts in Niebuhr's mind was the revolt against left-wing, progressive, advanced theology. His first movement was a movement to the right.

2

Movement to the Right

ONE of the most remarkable features of contemporary intellectual life both in England and the United States has been the tendency of the most penetrating social critics of our civilization to move from a left position in theology to the right, from liberalism to orthodoxy. Outstanding examples in England are Father Vidler and Canon Demant; continental examples are Karl Barth and Nicholas Berdyaev. The outstanding American example is Reinhold Niebuhr. Among Christian theologians, the profounder the thought, the more thorough-going is the movement away from liberalism to orthodoxy. The same tendency, in a different form, is observable among non-Christian thinkers. In their case, it is a movement from secular rationalism toward a religious hypothesis; an instance is Mr. Aldous Huxley. Christian liberalism was partly the expression and partly the creator of the simple delusion that it is within the power of human nature to create Utopia; that men, in fact, could be made Christian by act of parliament and other institutional, social action. The tendency, therefore, was for liberals in theology to become socialists in politics, with the idea that by implementing a socialist programme society would

30

be made Christian. That is to say, socialism was the practical embodiment of a theoretical Christianity.

Now when events began to reveal the hollowness of this too rosy assumption; when it came to be seen that social and technical progress was accompanied by a most distressing development of hitherto unsuspected evils, there emerged the beginnings of a new skepticism about the capacity of human nature, which was stimulated by the new psychologies of the unconscious. It was this skepticism that proved to be the point of departure in a new theological development toward the right, a reaction, in fact, in the proper meaning of the word. The dawning suspicion that technical progress might not, after all, prove to be a straight road to Utopia was the *terminus a quo* for a profound and widespread revolt against the whole attitude of Christian, or Protestant, liberalism and for a return to orthodoxy, especially to orthodox doctrine of sin. The hinge on which this whole movement turned was in Niebuhr's case the Reformation doctrine of justification by faith, which may truthfully be described as the "bovrilization" of the whole scheme of Christian sociology. It is the formulation in theological terms of man's social, secular development. One of the most considerable services of Niebuhr to contemporary Christian thinking has been the investing of theology, and more particularly this doctrine of justification by faith, with secular urgency. In the struggle for the correct appreciation of this dogma, Niebuhr has not spent his energies on remote, abstract, ghostly issues which move only in a transcendent realm, but on issues which, though tran-

scendent, also fatally affect the historically decisive
problems of power, progress and social justice.

At this point it is necessary to draw the reader's attention to a most significant feature in Niebuhr's development as a Christian revolutionary. It is this: in
the movement away from liberal theology Niebuhr did
not at the same time jettison the social criticism associated with the theology he was abandoning; he did
not throw away the baby with the bath-water. Indeed,
the more right he became in theology, the more left he
tended to become in politics. What was really happen-
ing was that his social criticism was becoming deeper,
more penetrating: it was turning into a criticism of
the ordinary left social criticism. He became acutely
aware of the fact that the political left shared the fundamental illusions of the political right. His social criticism thus took on a deeper hue. It acquired a new
motivation, a new dimension of perspective, which, in
time, led him to a distinctive Christian idea, which I
may define as the theory of the historically permanent
revolution—which will occupy us in the final chapter.

In this double development, Niebuhr was displaying
an essential characteristic of Christian thinking. He
was, in other words, preserving the permanent essence
of a temporary phase of development. In abandoning
the old, outworn idea he nevertheless preserved the
effect on his mentality and attitude of having under-
gone the process of thinking the old idea. A very important point, and a comparatively rare accomplish-
ment. That is why so many rebels of twenty-one become
tories at fifty or sixty. It is because of their inability

to preserve the ethos, the atmosphere of the idea when, at last, they abandon the idea itself. They become as though they had never thought an earlier phase at all— which is disintegration at its worst. It is almost inevitable, if a man grows at all, that he should outgrow the left illusions of his rebellious youth, though many of the typical secular left never do: in their old age they are still milling out the ideas and illusions of their callow youth. In a profound sense the whole secular left, with its tendency to totalitarianism, is a case of arrested development, not a second childhood but the perpetuation of the first childhood. Niebuhr has escaped this peril of arrested development, and also the peril of a supine drift into "traditionalism," in other words, of becoming a tory at fifty-five. From his continuous spiritual and intellectual growth he extracts the historic essence of the ideas which he no longer can accept as valid. Thus, at the pending transition from youth to age, he is a responsible revolutionary, in whom tradition and progress organically interpenetrate. This achievement has its root in his appropriation of the supreme contribution of the Protestant reformers—justification by faith.

* * *

From the stubborn and baffling contradiction of human experience and history it was perhaps inevitable that Niebuhr should turn to the Reformation doctrine. Inheriting as he did through his family history the traditions of the Reformation, it was not an accident that he should find the key to the perplexities and problems,

which his daily experience and thinking imposed upon
him, in the confession of his church. The point here
is that it was his social passion that dictated his theological development. His theology took shape under
the pressure of social and economic issues. He did not
become a theologian through the study of systematic
theology as an insulated, isolated activity. He acquired
his theology piece by piece, so to speak, as social issues awoke in his mind the need for fundamental foot-
hold. Niebuhr's theological development began in his
attempt to find some satisfactory answer to the abysmal
problems of human nature. And of all the great Christian dogmas, justification by faith is the one most directed to human nature. In this dogma lie the seeds of
every other great Christian doctrine. It implies a whole
system of theology. In it, potentially, are also the doctrines of sin and forgiveness, of providence and judgment, of divine creation and human freedom, all of
which Niebuhr personally came to realize under the
pressure of a growing social problem. He made the
paradoxical discovery that the firmest foundation for
radical politics was a conservative theology, that tradition was the surest safeguard of rational progress.

One of the first problems to oppress him was the terrible contrast between "moral man and immoral society," between the relatively decent, good behavior of
man as an individual, and man as a society, man in the
mass. It was a problem which defined a problem. The
fact of the contrast revealed to Niebuhr what he came
to regard as the basic problem of human nature in historical development. His analysis of this contrast led

him to the roots of the contradiction of human nature.

"Individual men may be moral in the sense that they are able to consider interests other than their own in determining problems of conduct, and are capable, on occasion, of preferring the advantages of others to their own. They are endowed by nature with a measure of sympathy and consideration for their kind, the breadth of which may be extended by an astute social pedagogy. Their rational faculty prompts them to a sense of justice which educational discipline may refine and purge of egoistic elements until they are able to view a social situation, in which their own interests are involved, with a fair measure of objectivity. But all these achievements are more difficult, if not impossible, for human societies and social groups. In every human group there is less reason to guide and to check impulse, less capacity for self-transcendence, less ability to comprehend the need of others and therefore more unrestrained egoism than the individuals, who compose the groups, reveal in their personal relationships" (*Moral Man and Immoral Society,* pp. xi–xii. Charles Scribner's Sons. Hereinafter referred to as M.M.).

In these words, Niebuhr states the fact of the morality of man the individual, and the immorality of man the collective, and in seeking to formulate and to solve this problem, he felt compelled to reject the too shallow assumptions about the power of reason to affect the force of egoism.

"In analyzing the limits of reason in morality it is important to begin by recognizing that the force of egoistic impulse is much more powerful than any but the most astute psychological analysts and the most rigorous devotees of introspection realize. If it is defeated on a lower or more obvious level, it will express itself in more subtle forms. If it is defeated by social impulse it insinuates itself into the social impulse, so that a man's devotion to his community always means the expression of a transferred egoism as well as of altruism. Reason may check egoism in order to fit it harmoniously into a total body of social impulse. But the same force of reason is bound to justify the egoism of the individual as a legitimate element in that total body of vital capacities, which society seeks to harmonize" (*op. cit.*, pp. 40–41).

Reason, in other words, becomes unconsciously the instrument of egoism. It becomes the agent of egoism under the impression that it is transcending it. There is the problem. It is this fatal, fundamental incapacity of reason which embodies itself in imperialism, in inflated materialism, in class exploitation, and also in proletarian resistance and in socialist power.

In this double power of reason, in its capacity to do opposite, contradictory things at the same time, Niebuhr discovered the clue to the problem of human nature. It lay in the fact that man existed in two dimensions of being. At one and the same time man was under the dominion of nature and also transcended nature. He was both in the realm of necessity and in the realm of freedom. He was both animal and spirit.

"The obvious fact is that man is child of nature, subject to its vicissitudes, compelled by its necessities, driven by its impulses, and confined within the brevity of the years which nature permits its varied organic forms, allowing them some, but not too much latitude. The other less obvious fact is that man is a spirit who stands outside of nature, life, himself, his reason and the world. This latter fact is appreciated in one or the other of its aspects by various philosophies. But it is not frequently appreciated in its total import. That man stands outside of nature in some sense is admitted even by naturalists who are intent upon keeping him as close to nature as possible. They must at least admit that he is *homo faber*, a tool-making animal. That man stands outside the world is admitted by naturalists who, with Aristotle, define man as a rational animal and interpret reason as the capacity for making general concepts. But the naturalists do not always understand that man's natural capacity involves a further ability to stand outside himself, a capacity for self-transcendence, the ability to make himself his own object, a quality of spirit which is usually not fully comprehended or connoted in *ratio* or *nous* or 'reason' or any of the concepts which philosophers usually use to describe the uniqueness of man" (*The Nature and Destiny of Man*. Vol. I, pp. 3–4. Charles Scribner's Sons. Hereinafter referred to as Gifford Lectures).

This analysis of the constitution of human nature in history is fundamental in Niebuhr's thought, since it involves for him the entire scheme of Christian orthodoxy. This two-dimensional existence of necessity and freedom, of nature and spirit, with its inevitable tension —the one dimension pulling one way and the other another way—constituted the environment for sin, on which the whole issue of man's historic existence turns.

"In short, man, being both free and bound, both limited and limitless, is anxious. Anxiety is the inevitable concomitant of the paradox of freedom and finiteness in which man is involved. Anxiety is the internal pre-condition of sin. It is the inevitable spiritual state of man, standing in the paradoxical situation of freedom and finiteness. Anxiety is the internal description of the state of temptation. It must not be identified with sin, because there is always the ideal possibility that faith would purge anxiety of the tendency towards sinful self-assertion. The ideal possibility is that faith in the ultimate security of God's love would overcome all immediate insecurities of nature and history. That is why Christian orthodoxy has consistently defined unbelief as the root of sin, or as the sin which precedes pride. . . . The freedom from anxiety which He [Christ] enjoins is a possibility only if perfect trust in divine security has been achieved. Whether such freedom from anxiety and such perfect trust are actual possibilities of historic existence must be considered later. For the present it is enough to observe that no life, even the most saintly, perfectly conforms to the injunction not to be anxious. . . . Yet anxiety is not sin. It must be distinguished from sin partly because it is its pre-condition and not its actuality, and partly because it is the basis of all human creativity as well as the pre-condition of sin. Man is anxious not only because his life is limited and dependent and yet not so limited that he does not know of his limitations. He is also anxious because he does not know the limits of his possibilities. He can do nothing and regard it perfectly done, because higher possibilities are revealed in each achievement. All human actions stand under seemingly limitless possibilities. There are, of course, limits but it is difficult to gauge them from any immediate perspective. There is therefore no limit of achievement in any sphere of activity in which human history can rest with equanimity" (Gifford Lectures, Vol. I, pp. 194–6).

In this state of anxiety, sin becomes a possibility, and the whole point about historic existence is that the possibility of sin has been actualized. Man is a sinner, which defines the contradiction of human nature and its prolonged and involved consequences in history. Niebuhr, more than any contemporary Christian theologian, has rehabilitated the Christian dogma of original sin in present-day thinking. He has done more than anyone of whom I have knowledge to rescue it from the neglect and contempt of a mere secular science and philosophy. He has done this, primarily, by revealing

its profound significance for sociology and the philosophy of history. Having seen the secret of the constitution of human nature in its two-fold dimension-
alism, he came to see social development as the
expression, the working-out, of the radical tension of
man's being as sin. Hence he looked upon the dogma
of original sin as fundamental in Christian theology
and as absolutely necessary for the interpretation of
the riddle of man's history. Once he saw the profound
significance of the dogma, he also came to see the ab-
surdity of its denial by liberal theology. " 'If we can't
find the real cause of social injustice,' said a typical
modern recently, 'we would be forced to go back to the
absurd doctrine of original sin.' That remark is a revelation of the scientific 'objectivity' of modernity. The
Christian idea of original sin is ruled out *a priori*. This
is understandable enough in a non-christian world.
What is absurd is that modern Christianity should have
accepted this modern rejection of the doctrine of original sin with such pathetic eagerness and should have
spent so much energy in seeking to prove that a Christian can be just as respectable and modern as a secular-
ist" (*Christianity and Power Politics*, pp. 36–7. Charles
Scribner's Sons). In rejecting original sin, liberalism
was, in effect, suppressing God's Good News to man.

Niebuhr realized that sin was the unique product of
man, the distinctive characteristic of self-consciousness.
It was not the survival of man's animal heritage. Sin
only becomes possible on the level of spirit. This discovery exposed the hollowness of the liberal vision of
historic progress.

"In place of it [the Genesis account of the origin of
evil] we have substituted various accounts of the
origin and the nature of evil in human life. Most of
these accounts, reduced to their essentials, attribute
sin to the inertia of nature, or the hypertrophy of
impulses, or to the defect of reason (ignorance), and
thereby either explicitly or implicitly place their trust
in developed reason as the guarantee of goodness.
In all of these accounts the essential point in the nature of human evil is incised, namely, that it arises
from the very freedom of reason with which man is
endowed. Sin is not so much a consequence of natural impulses, which in animal life do not lead to sin,
as of the freedom by which man is able to throw the
harmonies of nature out of joint. He disturbs the
harmony of nature when he centers his life about one
particular impulse (sex or the possessive impulse, for
instance) or when he tries to make himself, rather
than God, the center of existence. This egoism is sin
in its quintessential form. It is not a defect of nature, but a defect which becomes possible because
man has been endowed with a freedom not known in
the rest of Creation" (*Beyond Tragedy,* pp. 10–11).

Niebuhr's emphasis upon the fact of sin and his analysis of its essential character is a decisive demonstration of the relation between his theology and his social
radicalism, of the fortifying of the Christian revolutionary by traditional doctrine. It illustrates how his
temperamental tendency to social revolution is sustained
by orthodox dogma; how, in fact, he was driven to

orthodox theology for the security of his revolutionary
impulse, so as to establish it on an immovable foundation. I will give one more extract from Niebuhr's work
which seems to me to prove this process beyond doubt.

"The truth is that, absurd as the classical Pauline
doctrine of original sin may seem to be at first blush,
its prestige as a part of the Christian truth is preserved, and perennially re-established, against the
attacks of rationalists and simple moralists by its
ability *to throw light upon complex factors in human behavior which constantly escape the moralists*
[My italics, D. R. D.]. It may be valuable to use a
simple example of contemporary history to prove the
point. Modern religious nationalism is obviously a
highly explicit expression of the collective pride in
which all human behavior is involved and which
Christian faith regards as the quintessence of sin.
In so far as this pride issues in specific acts of cruelty,
such as the persecution of the Jews, these acts obviously cannot be defined as proceeding from a de-
liberate and malicious preference for evil in defiance
of the good. It is true of course that a modern dev-
otee of the religions of race and nation regards his
nation as the final good more deliberately than a
primitive tribalist, who merely assumed that his collective life was the end of existence. Yet it would be
fallacious to assume that a nazi gives unqualified
devotion to the qualified and continued value of his
race and nation by a consciously perverse choice of
the lesser against the higher good. But it would be

equally erroneous to absolve the religious nationalist of responsibility merely because his choice is not consciously perverse" (Gifford Lectures, Vol. I, p. 264).

In his endeavor to understand the social problem and, consequently, to pursue action about it more effectively, we see that Niebuhr was compelled to become a theologian. From his analysis of human nature he proceeded to the fact of sin, more particularly original sin, which afforded him insights into the social situation that inevitably led him still further to the right theologically. Reflection on this total fact of sin illumined for him the meaning and inner significance of another stubborn, tragic fact—the fact of revolutionary frustration, which may be expressed in two ways. First, that social change never realizes the aims and intentions of its advocates, that, in fact, it frequently results in the opposite. Second, that social change, when the new situation has crystallized and settled, frequently gives rise to other objects which side-track and overlay the original aims. This always happens both on the big historic scale, in mass revolutionary movements, and in the smaller collective conflicts of groups, parties and movements. Original sin gave Niebuhr the clue to the correct interpretation of this persistent phenomenon, so calamitous in its results. The understanding of this, in turn, did something of incalculable importance for Niebuhr the revolutionary. It delivered him from undue illusions about the process of social development. The significance of this fact for Niebuhr's development cannot be exaggerated.

He defined sin, as we have seen, as centralization of
the ego. The generic term in which this whole process
is summed up is *pride*. Anxiety is the soil in which it
grows. Lack of trust in God leads to the desire to assume control of one's own being—and that is affirmation of self as central and dominant. This pride then
operates as a continuously corrupting element in every
human situation, but more especially in collective, institutional development. Whilst in the new social forms,
the institutional evils of the displaced social order are
destroyed, the corrupting element of sin in the human
beings in the new order continues to bedevil all social
relationships, and consequently tends to frustrate revolutionary hopes and aspirations. This is one of the most
constant and basic themes in all Niebuhr's writing and
thinking.

> "They [Marxists] imagine that social peace will re-
> sult from the victory of one class over all other
> classes. They have not taken into account that mod-
> ern capitalism produces a formidable middle class the
> interests of which are not identical with the prole-
> tarians. Moral and spiritual considerations may con-
> ceivably prompt this class to make common cause
> with the workers in the attainment of ethical social
> ends, but it will never be annihilated even by the most
> ruthless class conflict nor will it be persuaded by the
> logic of economic facts that its interests are alto-
> gether identical with those of the workers. Even if
> one class were able to eliminate all other classes,
> which is hardly probable, it would require some social

grace and moral dynamic to preserve harmony between the various national groups by which this vast
mass would be organized and into which it would
disintegrate. Even within one national unit any economic class will dissolve into various groups, according to varying and sometimes conflicting interests as soon as its foes are eliminated. The Russian communists were not long able to preserve their
absolute solidarity after their revolution was firmly
established" (*Does Civilization Need Religion?* pp.
146–7. Charles Scribner's Sons).

This frustration of the social process by the corrupting element of sin inevitably posed the problem of
whether frustration also meant futility. If human hope
and aspiration are constantly subject to a process of
frustration, isn't history reduced to futility? Isn't the
Golden City of man's dream in that case a mirage? If
all that the social process does is to create new forms
of injustice, what can be the point of it all? Inspiration
to pursue the goal is dependent upon illusion, upon
ignorance or unawareness of the character of human
nature. When illusion is dissipated, when at last there
comes realization of the corrupting element at work in
man and his institutions, and the consequent impotence
of the human will, inspiration surely dries up, and there
follows a paralysis of the will-to-struggle.

That conclusion is inevitable if time and history constitute the one and only arena of human struggle and
achievement, and if man has only his own power to depend on for the realization of social justice. If these

two propositions are true, then we can write over the portals of time what Dante inscribed on the portals of Hell: "Abandon hope all ye who enter here." Thus moral and social realism demands; if revolution is to be effective, the existence of another dimension, another order of being. It demands a world transcending time, if social development is to find ultimate fulfillment. And it also demands some power other than the human will, if the corrupting element in history is to be finally overcome. Hence final realization must be the result of some reality over and above the process of development. It was exactly at this point that Niebuhr saw the profound relevance of the theological ideas and language of the great Christian doctrines, especially of justification by faith, to the whole of human history. Justification by faith affirms that the contradiction of human nature is overcome, not by historic development, but by divine action, by the free grace of God. The great classic theological terms, "reconciliation," "forgiveness," "grace," take on sociological significance. Social change and revolution are finally validated by faith in divine forgiveness. On the sure foundation of this massive dogma, moral realism and social revolution join hands. Realism strengthens and intensifies revolution.

"Mere development of what he now is cannot save man, for development will heighten all the contradictions in which he stands. Nor will emancipation from the law of development and the march of time through entrance into a timeless and motionless

eternity save him. His hope consequently lies in a
forgiveness which will overcome not his finiteness
but his sin, and a divine omnipotency which will
complete his life without destroying its essential nature. Hence the final expression of hope in the
Apostolic Creed, 'I believe in the forgiveness of sins,
the resurrection of the body and the life everlasting,'
is a much more sophisticated expression of hope in
ultimate fulfillment than all of its modern substitutes.
It grows out of a realization of the total human situation which the modern mind has not fathomed. The
symbols by which this hope is expressed are, to be
sure, difficult. The modern mind imagines that it has
rejected the hope because of this difficulty. But the
real cause of the rejection lies in its failure to understand the problem of human existence in all its complexity" (*Beyond Tragedy,* p. 306). In short, it lies
in the continued entertaining by the modern mind of
the illusion of human power.

We are perhaps in a better position now to appreci-
ate the paradox that Niebuhr had to move to the right
theologically, if he was to continue politically and so-
cially left. It was orthodox theology that saved him,
once he became realist, from secular cynicism, which
is camouflaged despair. Only a theologically orthodox
Christian can continue to be a revolutionary without
illusions about human nature and the historic process.
Niebuhr is one of the rare company that tries to follow
Matthew Arnold's friend, who "saw life steadily, and
saw it whole." He can do that in virtue of the power

and insight he derives from his Christian faith and theology. "They that wait upon the Lord shall renew their strength . . . they shall walk, and *not faint*."

* * *

Since this study is in no sense an attempt to estimate the place of Niebuhr as a theologian, but purely as a Christian revolutionary, as one seeking to bring about fundamental social change as much as possible in accordance with Christianity, I am not endeavoring to give an account of his theology as a system. I summarize it in as far as it is a direct factor in his social attitude—which is very far indeed. So far the vital influence of theology upon his revolutionary activity is summed up, as we have already argued, in the doctrine of justification by faith, which has been discussed simply for its sociological significance. This is not to say that Niebuhr is concerned with that doctrine only for its sociology. That would be a perverse misrepresentation of his position. The Reformers rested the whole weight of the destiny of the individual upon that doctrine, and so does Niebuhr, as a study of his Gifford lectures amply and clearly demonstrates. But here we are engaged only upon its application to a social problem. It solved for him the baffling problem of the contradiction of man's situation in history. We have now to examine how Niebuhr solved the problem of making revolution significant, of the relation between historic frustration and spiritual fulfillment. This involves the whole problem of the destiny of man both as individual and society, which presents itself first as the question: What is the final purpose of the whole historic process?

This is the point at which the first great distinction emerges between the Christian revolutionary and the secular revolutionary; between, shall we say, Lenin and Niebuhr. It is but rarely that secular revolutionary theory takes any account of ultimate problems, of questions of final destiny. Neither Marx nor Engels ever got nearer to them than vague, romantic generalizations.

The question of final destiny which is never explicitly formulated in secular theory must, therefore, be sought for in the implications of theory. The concrete historical situations envisaged by secular revolutionaries, particularly by Marx and Engels, imply, at every point, an *unformulated* view of final destiny, between which and the consciously, systematically defined Christian view there is a gulf, which no amount of desperate "interpenetration of opposites" by Christian Marxists (that strange breed!) can ever bridge. But it seems that the following affirmations can be justly made about the secular-revolutionary view of final purpose.

(*a*). At its best—and it is by its best it should be judged—the final purpose of this vision seems to be the maximum development of the personal gifts and talents of the individual personality. The secular revolutionary conceives a system of society which will give opportunity for the individual to achieve full self-expression, to develop all of which he is capable. Society is the highest reality (or entity) of human existence. Secular-revolutionary theory never looks beyond mankind. Self-realization is the goal of evolution.

(*b*). The realization of this final purpose will be effected within time and history. In this view, time is an absolute.

Niebuhr's opposition to all this was so radical that it involved all the essentials of orthodox Christian eschatology. In effect, he found in the orthodox doctrines of "the last things" his philosophy of history, so much so in fact that they constituted the keystone, the essential idea, of his whole system of belief. Speaking of the rejection, in his student days, of the doctrine of the resurrection of the body and of the theological changes in subsequent years, he writes, "Yet some of us have been persuaded to take the stone which we then rejected and make it the head of the corner. In other words, there is no part of the Apostolic Creed which, in our present opinion, expresses the whole genius of the Christian faith more neatly than just this despised phrase: 'I believe in the resurrection of the body' " (*op. cit.*, p. 290).

The supreme purpose of the historic process in the secular view becomes, according to Niebuhr, a by-product, so to speak, the fruit or consequence of another, prior purpose. Christianity teaches that man's chief purpose is to glorify God, to be obedient to his will, to be in perfect filial fellowship with him. An effect of that fellowship with God, the relationship to him, is that men will enjoy self-realization. The satisfaction for which the human ego craves in its artificial centrality is to be found only in a relationship of subordination to and dependence upon God. "Seek ye first the kingdom of God and his righteousness, and all these things shall be added unto you." Seek first the right relationship to God, out of which self-realization will come as a spontaneous, organic growth; give "glory to God in the highest," not "glory to man in the highest." Modern civilization is, in fact, the attempt to create by independent human will what the Kingdom of God grants to a mankind rightly dependent upon God.

The complete realization of this purpose for all mankind lies beyond time and history altogether. The fulfillment of the historic process is beyond history. This view is fundamental in all Niebuhr's thinking. On no theme is he more profound in his thought or more eloquent in his statement. It is here, too, that the cleavage between Christian revolutionary theory and secular theory is evident and deepest; where the two attitudes are utterly irreconcilable. History is inevitably an arena of frustration, of incompleteness. The goal of all human striving lies in another dimension. History, in its totality, moves toward the end, in the sense of *finis,* as history, in its successive phases, ends. But the final end (*finis*) of history will also, says Niebuhr, be identified with the end as fulfillment, *telos.* The essential affirmation of orthodox Christian eschatology is that the end of history (as *finis*) will coincide with the end as *telos,* fulfillment. "The culmination of history must include not merely the divine completion of human incompleteness but a purging of human guilt and sin by divine judgment and mercy."

The Kingdom of God is itself the fulfillment of history, which is apprehended in secular thought by partial and distorting conceptions and ideas, such as "an age of plenty," "perpetual world peace," "brotherhood of man," "world federation," "classless society." These, in fact, are the expression of the fundamental human sin of "the very effort of men to solve this problem by their own resources." But the Kingdom of God has already come into history in Christ. The end of history (as *telos*) has preceded the end as *finis*. This is the supreme paradox of Christian faith. ". . . the Kingdom of God as it *has come* in Christ means a disclosure of the meaning of history but not the full realization of that meaning. That is anticipated in the Kingdom which *is to come,* that is, in the culmination of history. It must be remembered that a comprehension of the meaning of life and history from the standpoint of the Christian revelation includes an understanding of the contradictions of that meaning in which history is perennially involved" (Gifford Lectures, Vol. II, pp. 297–8).

Niebuhr comprehends the fulfillment of the whole historic process in the threefold biblical symbolism of the *Parousia* (the second coming of Christ), the Last Judgment, and the Resurrection, which he has systematically discussed in the second volume of his Gifford lectures (pages 297 to 332). Here one can attempt but the briefest summary.

The Parousia. In the hope of the return of Christ is affirmed the *ultimate* identity of righteousness and power, that in the end God will overcome all evil. It is the assertion of the conviction that the love of God is omnipotent. In the process of historic development, the omnipotence of love manifests itself as power to endure the defiance of sin. But that same power to endure will, in the end (*finis* and *telos*) reveal itself as power

to abolish and dissipate sin. That is to say, the final dis-
appearance of sin will be the logical conclusion of the
endurance of sin in time and history. Capacity to endure in history becomes power to banish in the end.
"The vindication of Christ and his triumphant return
is therefore an expression of faith in the sufficiency of
God's sovereignty over the world and history, and in
the final supremacy of love over all the forces of self-
love which defy, for the moment, the inclusive harmony of all things under the will of God." There will
come a point at which the principle of contradiction in
history, by which all new achievements in human order
are corrupted and disputed, will be overcome. There
will come a point—I use this word "point" rather than
the word "moment" or "time"—when justice will cease
to breed new injustice, when "all things according well
shall make one music as before."

The Last Judgment. The Last Judgment, says Niebuhr, enshrines three basic ideas of the Christian philosophy of history. It states that since Christ himself
will be the judge, history will be judged by the ideal
possibility which has already been known in history.
On this point he quotes Augustine so strikingly that I
cannot forbear quoting in turn: "God the Father will in
his [Christ's] personal presence judge no man, but he
has given his judgment to his Son who shall show himself *as a man* to judge the world, even as he showed
himself as a man to be judged of the world." History
in its totality, will be judged by the absolute possibility
which man perceived in the relative situations of historic development. It will be finally evaluated, judged

—*i.e.,* admitted as true—by the "ought," by the ideal possibility which, though appearing in history, nevertheless always stood above history. The Last Judgment, that is to say, will be congruent with the manifestations of historic judgment.

The second of the basic ideas is the justification of the historic distinction between good and evil. While the particular relative distinctions between right and wrong may have been confused and unjust in the actual historical situation, that there was an actual distinction to be made will become manifest in the culmination of history. In social revolution, the interests of transcendent righteousness paradoxically join hands with egocentric interests *for a time,* so that the revolutionary is (mostly) an unconscious instrument of Providence. The distinction between good and evil in the actual concrete situation, however partially and wrongly its content may be perceived, is nevertheless absolute. Hence the Last Judgment affirms that the historic process is essentially moral. "Morality is the nature of things" (Bishop Butler).

The third idea symbolized in the Last Judgment is the denial of any possibility that history can fulfill or complete itself. The achievements of history, its progressions, do not constitute stages, so to speak, of the Kingdom of God. The historic process is not the Kingdom of God by installments. Each stage or installment is marred by the corrupting element of man's self-affirmation. Fulfillment comes from God at the end, yet is nevertheless related to the whole process of history. The Last Judgment is the unambiguous, absolute af-

firmation of man's incapacity to fulfill history himself.

> *Our little systems have their day,*
> *They have their day and cease to be.*
> *They are but broken lights of Thee*
> *And Thou, O Lord, art more than they.*

A "broken light" gives sufficient light, not to see, but to
"mis-see." It gives a semi-darkness in which objects are
distorted to the vision. "Now we see as in a glass,
darkly." "The idea of a 'Last' Judgment expresses
Christianity's refutation of all conceptions of history,
according to which it is its own redeemer and is able
by the process of growth and development to emanci-
pate man from the guilt and sin of his existence, and
to free him from judgment."

The Resurrection. The symbolism of the resurrection
of the body is, undoubtedly, the one which has called
forth the greatest contempt of the modern secular mind,
and the one about which liberal Christianity has felt
most ashamed. Niebuhr insists that it is a symbol, which
like all other symbols, can be made to appear ridiculous
when clothed in a rational form. But its significance is
profound; for it affirms nothing less than the redemption of history in its entirety. What will be validated
is the whole man, the unity of body and spirit, not man
levitated into a bloodless soul merely. "On the one hand,
it [the Resurrection] implies that eternity will fulfill
and not annul the richness and variety which the
temporal process has elaborated. On the other hand it
implies that the condition of finiteness and freedom,

which lies at the basis of historical existence, is a problem for which there is no solution by any human power. Only God can solve this problem." This symbol affirms, in other words, that nothing gained in historical development will be wasted or lost, which is what happens in history only too frequently. The predominant personal relationships of feudal society have been almost entirely lost in capitalist society. As Marx puts it so eloquently in the Communist Manifesto, "Wherever the bourgeoisie has risen to power, it has destroyed all feudal, patriarchal, and idyllic relationships. . . . It has degraded personal dignity to the level of exchange value." And as the Marxists have *not* said, socialist society, if Russia is any criterion, will throw away the capitalist gain of individual liberty. The symbol of the resurrection of the body states a law of the moral uniformity of historical development—that no value gained in the process will be lost "or cast as rubbish to the void."

* * *

Thus Niebuhr, in his endeavor to validate the radical, revolutionary attitude, discovered that he had to move to the right. The great slogan in America in the early nineteenth century was "Go west, young man." The slogan uttered to Niebuhr by the spirit of prophecy was "Go 'right,' young man," which he did, as we have seen, with a vengeance. His movement rightwards had startling results in that it made of him a very rare kind of revolutionary, as we shall endeavor to see more fully in the concluding part of this study. He was, in all probability, a revolutionary by instinct; to put it in the language of religion, a revolutionary by a divine call. In order to remain where he was—on the left—he had to go right. On the impregnable foundation of a traditional theology, he has reared a revolutionary social theory. By a profound biblical Christian dialectic, his movement to the right involved him in a movement to the left—but the left on to which he moved differed "more than somewhat" from the left of secular theory.

3

Movement to the Left

IT HAS become a commonplace to say nowadays that
there can be no revolution without a theory. Part of
the greatness of Lenin was his realization of this simple
but dramatic necessity which Marx first made clear.
Marx's jibe at Bakunin, the old Russian anarchist, has
become famous. Bakunin, he said, was always mistak-
ing the third month (of the pregnancy of the revolution) for the ninth. Bakunin lacked a theory. Lenin, on
the contrary, correctly diagnosed the existence of a
revolutionary situation in 1917, though he was the only
one to do so.[1]

Whether Marxist theory is an infallible guide to rec-
ognition of the revolutionary "moment" is, at least,
arguable. But there can be no doubt that the first job of
the revolutionary is interpretation of events as elements
in a developing situation. And this is pre-eminently
what Niebur does. Is it fantastic to suggest that the
word "revolutionary" is a translation into secular ter-
minology of the religious, theological word "prophet"?
And is "revolutionary theory" a secular version of

---

[1] My friend J. T. Murphy, who knew Lenin well, once told me
that Lenin said to him that "he was in a minority of one" in his
insistence that the moment for the seizure of power by the bol-
sheviks had arrived in October 1917.

"prophetic insight"? There is much to suggest that Marx's theory was much more the product of his heart than his head; that its service was prophetic rather than rational. It was insight much more than it was ratiocination. It is certain, however, that Niebuhr reveals extraordinary insight into the meaning of events in our time, and that interpretation of the social situation constitutes a very large and profoundly important part of his activities as a Christian revolutionary. And as an interpreter, he is certainly far to the left of conventional ecclesiastical judgment of affairs.

Rather than attempt a summary of Niebuhr's social and political judgments, which would inevitably be colorless and bald, let me endeavor to define the *principles* of these judgments, which perhaps will illustrate his move to the left more satisfactorily. With the aid of these principles, readers can then turn to Niebuhr's books; for the only justification of such a study as this is to direct the reader to Niebuhr himself.[2]

I would formulate these principles thus: (*a*) The relative character of all historical situations and judgments; (*b*) The absolute (or eternal) significance of the relative historical situation.

---

[2] Whilst everything that Niebuhr writes exemplifies his social and political theory, I may instance as particularly relevant the following: *Reflections on the End of an Era, Christianity and Power Politics, Moral Man and Immoral Society.* The reader should also pay attention to chapters four, five and six of *An Interpretation of Christian Ethics* and the second volume of the Gifford lectures. His editorials in the quarterly journal of the Fellowship of Socialist Christians, *Christianity and Society,* are also of first-class importance.

Consistent with the dialectical quality of all Niebuhr's thinking, these two principles partake of the nature of paradox, and comprehend, in essence, the entire field of his application of Christian faith to society.

* * *

First, then, the relative character of all historical situations and judgments.

One of the abiding common characteristics of all secular revolutionaries is the tendency to think of their own revolutionary achievement as final. They tend to lose any awareness—if they ever possessed it—that their achievement partakes fully of the defect and partiality of all historic movements. They never think that their creation will ever have to be undone; they assume that their aims, when at last they are realized, have a final significance for history. In other words, their revolutionary achievements are an absolute gain for the class or society they represent. Revolutionaries hardly ever manifest any doubts about the significance of their achievements, which henceforth become something to be exploited to the maximum of their power. Having conquered, their triumph has but to be applied. They harbor no doubts about the adequacy of the instrument for the realization of the aims to which they have devoted themselves. We never find, on the morrow of successful revolution, that the revolutionary shows any awareness that his very success may be the beginning of defeat of his purpose.

Now this psychology of the secular revolutionary is natural and almost inevitable. It is beyond the power of

human nature to doubt the thing to which it is most
passionately committed. How can we expect men who
have suffered and endured everything for their cause to
believe that, in the triumph of that for which they have
labored, is concealed the seed of frustration and defeat? If revolutionary human nature were capable of
rising to such heights of objectivity, history would have
developed very differently. But it is clear that revolutions never realize purely the aim of their architects. In
every revolutionary triumph there is a corrupting element at work, which frequently ordains that the revolution becomes an instrument to defeat its own original
aims. It destroys historic forms only to embody the
content, the substance of the old forms in new historic
forms. The French Revolution certainly destroyed the
bonds of feudal society. But it most certainly did not
achieve its threefold aim in a single one of its particu-
lars. Bourgeois inequalities replaced feudal inequalities.

Now the outstanding characteristic of Niebuhr as a
revolutionary is his awareness of precisely this omni-
present element of corruption in the whole historic
process and therefore in revolutionary movements. All
revolutionaries can sense this element in the movements
which they oppose. The greatness of Niebuhr is that
he senses it in the movements which he champions.
There can be no doubt that, on the whole, Niebuhr is
fundamentally more in sympathy with Marxism than
with liberalism, in spite of the shock which Soviet policies since 1935 have occasioned him. But he is as clearly
aware of the corruption in Marxism as he is of that in
liberalism. His awareness of this element is so acute

that he detects its operation in all movements of emancipation, with which movements his sympathies and pas-
sions overwhelmingly lie. In his *Reflections on the End
of an Era* (Charles Scribner's Sons) he says:

> "The executors of judgment in history are always
> driven by both hunger and dreams, by both the pas-
> sions of warfare and the hope for a city of God.
> . . . To put the matter in terms of specific history:
> The cruelties of Czardom are avenged by the furor
> of a communism which so mixes creative and moral
> elements in its enterprise with so many primeval pas-
> sions and so many of the old cruelties inverted that
> only a very objective and sympathetic observer can
> discern what is good in the welter or what is evil.
> It must therefore always be the purpose of those who
> try, in a measure, to guide the course of history to
> check the desperate brutalities of a dying civilization
> in order that the new which emerges may not be too
> completely corrupted and blinded by the spirit of
> vengeance. . . . In brief, the judges of history are
> always barbarians, whether they be Teutonic hordes,
> beating at the gates of Rome, medieval tradesmen
> and townsmen whose commercial argosies destroyed
> the power of the lord in his castle, or modern prole-
> tarians, intent on an equalitarian and collectivist so-
> ciety."

In short, whilst Niebuhr is objectively committed to
one side in the social conflict, he, nevertheless, is sub-
jectively impartial in that he is clearly aware of the

corrupting element at work in both sides of the revolutionary debate.

The thoroughness of Niebuhr's prophetic perception in this respect is proved by his clear-eyed criticism of the churches in their judgment in social problems. He is unsparing in his vision of the Protestant and Roman Catholic Churches alike. The great source of self-deception in the churches, according to Niebuhr, lies precisely in their too simple judgments, in their failure to perceive the relative character of every historical situation, including their own. Every affirmation of Christianity in social action is partial, relative and mixed, in that it is compounded of some vested interest of the Church. It was on this ground that he criticized the Vatican in its apparent attitude to the civil war in Spain. Niebuhr vigorously exposed the claim that Franco and the rebels were defending Christianity. The elements of power and vested property interests were too mixed up with a genuine concern for Christian faith to admit of so simple a judgment. In a similar way, he criticizes the varieties of Protestant Christianity, of which his analysis of Buchmanism is as good an example as any. "The Oxford Group Movement," he writes, "imagining itself the mediator of Christ's salvation in a catastrophic age, is really an additional evidence of the decay in which we stand. Its religion manages to combine bourgeois complacency with Christian contrition in a manner which makes the former dominant. Its morality is a religious expression of a decadent individualism. Far from offering us a way out

of our difficulties it adds to the general confusion. This
is not the Gospel's message of judgment and hope to
the world. It is bourgeois optimism, individualism and
moralism expressing itself in the guise of religion"
(*Christianity and Power Politics,* p. 156).

The conclusion at which Niebuhr arrives is that final
solutions of social problems are impossible in human
history. All solutions are necessarily partial, incomplete
and dynamically imperfect. That is to say, every solution, whether achieved by revolutionary means or not,
gives rise to a new form of the particular problem.
Every historical situation is relative. It always remains
under the judgment of the absolute ideal, which defies
every attempt at complete incarnation.

Revolutionaries have always been intolerant. But it
makes all the difference in the world whether intolerance is looked upon and felt as a virtue or a sin. If it
be regarded as a virtue the corrupting element in every
revolution operates without check or inhibition. If it
is felt to be a sin, then the corrupting element operates
under some sort of control. Now the great historic significance of Niebuhr's insight into the relativity of all
historical situations and judgments is precisely that it
brings this tendency to intolerance and its consequent
brutality under moral judgment. Revolutions, of which
there is going to be a rich crop in the post-war world,
will be less likely to stultify their historic mission if the
revolutionaries who engineer and guide them will be
men laboring under a sense of guilt for their extravagance and intolerance. Europe will suffer less if its
future explosions are in the hands of Cromwells rather

than Lenins or Stalins. Can anyone imagine Stalin, for instance, saying "I beseech you, comrades, in the bowels of The Dialectic, think it possible you may be mistaken"? Given this insight, which is characteristic of Niebuhr's whole attitude, revolutionaries would acquire a sense of guilt—to the infinite blessing of a tortured humanity.

* * *

There is, secondly, the opposite principle: Every relative historical situation has an absolute significance. In other words, no judgment of a historical situation is adequate, unless it is viewed against the background of an order higher than history. History cannot be fully interpreted in terms only of itself.

Niebuhr came to understand that it is Christian theology which alone makes history rational; that if the meaning of history is to be sought only within the historic process itself, then it is just meaningless. A dispassionate survey of the history of civilizations, whatever else it may do, cannot possibly fortify optimism or faith in the possibility of final achievement. Historic development is, among other things, a terrible process of disillusionment and frustration of man's hopes and dreams. We might consider the example of war. So far from being a modern dream, the vision of a warless world is one of the most ancient in human thought, and persists in face of cumulative disappointment. All the great wars in modern history have been, in the minds of the people, wars to end war. That was the promise of the French revolutionary wars. But nearly 3,000 years ago a great prophet and reformer saw a world in which swords had been beaten into plowshares, and every man enjoyed the security of his own home and work. Three thousand years are a very long time. If human hope is to be sustained—so one would assume—wars during that period should have declined both in frequency and intensity, even if they had not disappeared. But in fact they have increased. 2,700 years after the prophet Micah dreamed his noble dream, we are beating our pots and pans into bombers. War is threatening to do today what it could not have done 3,000 years ago— destroy whole communities and nations. Looking at the story of war and peace in terms of history alone does not encourage belief in the possibility of universal peace, but the exact opposite. If history be the only sphere, Moltke was quite right: peace *is* a dream. The tired waves which vainly break on the shores of man's existence in time and space not only do not *seem* their painful inch to gain; they do not, *in fact,* gain an inch. On the contrary, they have receded miles. The contemplation of history alone paralyzes the will. If 3,000 years of struggling, preaching, propaganda result in bigger and more frequent wars, what hope can one reasonably entertain—if history be the only factor?

The situation is no more encouraging if we think of human happiness and welfare in general: we have only to contrast the reality of today with past anticipations. If history is man's only reference, how bleak the prospect, how utterly meaningless the whole story: to fight, to create, to toil, to dream—that at the end we may compete with the Gadarene swine in the swiftness of descent. If history be the boundary of man's vision, there is no inspiration whatever to spur men on in revolutionary struggle.

Niebuhr, as well as seeing the partial, relative character of history, sees the passing situation, with all its contradiction, against a super-historic background. This vision he derives from Christian orthodoxy. His revolutionary spirit is fed by theology. The frustrations, stultifications, denials of historic development are all disciplinary elements in a fulfillment beyond time altogether. Given this hope of a transcendent fulfillment, the historic, the time-process becomes meaningful. Its irrationality becomes the overtone of an undercurrent rational theme. Hence there is value in the *process,* and not only in the goal. Man can travel hopefully.

Niebuhr's theological view of the historic process as having absolute significance is fortified by the fact that, where it is denied, one of two things happens. Either some substitute view is attempted as an inferior equivalent, or man falls back on materialism in sheer despair. Marx, of course, denied altogether the Christian hope of transcendental fulfillment. He is therefore compelled to anticipate fulfillment in time, which he does, not on scientific historical evidence (which is hostile), but on myth or "faith." He assumes the inevitability of historic fulfillment. In fact, however, Marx's conclusion disappears into non-history. When at long last the state will have withered away, class conflict will cease altogether and with it will go the famous dialectic. Communist society will have no tension. But this is not history. It is eschatology transposed into the time-key. The

secular alternative to this is crude, vitalistic materialism, of which Spengler affords a fitting example in his
learned but meretricious *Decline of The West* wherein,
confining himself to history, he is driven to the appalling conclusion that civilization is the blind expression of power. All anti-theological interpretations of
historic development are a variation (with modifica-
tion) on either secularized eschatology or on the crud-
est materialist vitalism. Marx, Spengler, Niebuhr—
these three names typify the varieties of the possible
views of historical meaning. Niebuhr's view of the absolute significance of the historical situation combines
realism toward the facts with a dynamic will to
struggle and to hope.

"Moral life is possible at all only in a meaningful
existence. Obligation can only be felt to some system
of coherence and some ordering will. Thus moral
obligation is always an obligation to promote harmony and to overcome chaos. But every conceivable
order in the historical world contains an element of
anarchy. Its world rests upon contingency and
caprice. The obligation to support and enhance it
can therefore only arise and maintain itself upon the
basis of a faith that it is the partial fruit of a deeper
unity and the promise of a more perfect harmony
than is revealed in any immediate situation. If a
lesser faith than this prompts moral action, it results
in precisely those types of moral fanaticism which
impart unqualified worth to qualified values and
thereby destroy their qualified worth. The prophetic

faith in a God who is both the ground and the ultimate fulfillment of existence, who is both the creator
and the judge of the world, is thus involved in every
moral situation. Without it the world is seen rather
to be meaningless or as revealing unqualifiedly good
and simple meanings. In either case, the nerve of
moral action is ultimately destroyed. The dominant
attitudes of prophetic faith are gratitude and contrition; gratitude for Creation and contrition before
Judgment; or, in other words, confidence that life
is good in spite of its evil and that it is evil in spite
of its good. In such a faith both sentimentality and
despair are avoided. The meaningfulness of life does
not tempt to premature complacency and the chaos
which always threatens the world of meaning does
not destroy the tension of faith and hope in which
all moral action is grounded" (*An Interpretation of
Christian Ethics,* pp. 115–16. Harper & Brothers).

In accordance with all Niebuhr's thinking, his movement toward the left is also dialectical—*i.e.,* it is a tension between two apparently opposite principles. First,
he denies the possibility of absolute achievement in any
historical situation, but, second, he nevertheless affirms
a more than relative significance in each historical situation, since his perception of the situation is in terms
of an order transcending it.

*   *   *

Niebuhr's "revolutionism" (may I be pardoned for
this word), which has driven him to the left in politics,
is a necessary consequence of his view that history is

dynamic, which again, in turn, is the result of his biblical view of the character of human nature. The core and essence of this view is that man is a unity of vitality and reason, which is the source of tension and conflict in all social relations. Urge and stimulus do not reside in reason, but in will, in the vitalities. Hence history can never "stay put." All achievements become the springboard for a new drive. Social growth *via* conflict is moralized as a struggle for justice. And it is as a champion of justice that Niebuhr has displayed his revolutionary attitude. The most important part of his activity in this respect is, in my judgment, his work as prophetic interpreter of the social scene, which he does through his books, his journalism, his preaching and lecturing in the United States and also here in Great Britain.

As Niebuhr came to theological clarity and maturity he found himself in a hostile environment—hostile in the sense that he was in opposition to the established theological and social traditions of the American churches. The United States was the land of the most strongly entrenched capitalism in the whole world. Many of the most powerful and wealthy capitalists were prominent church members, whose work was largely financed by the big contributions and bequests of these capitalists. This fact was a considerable influence in the formation of the individualist and capitalist character of American Christianity. "Where your treasure is, there will your heart be also." It is most difficult to be objective toward institutions on which we depend for our income and existence. Besides, the United States

had come to full national self-consciousness and greatness through the capitalist system and ideology, which
had been immensely strengthened by the fact of the
frontier—"America was a land of limitless opportunity
for everybody." All this was reflected in the predomi-
nantly liberal, optimist theology of the American Protestant churches. However divided they were on matters
of doctrine, order and ritual, they were pretty well at
one in their social outlook. It was this outlook to which
Niebuhr found himself in opposition.

It speaks volumes for the reality of democratic freedom in the United States that Niebuhr could publicly
criticize the fundamentals of American social Christianity and, at the same time, be invited to occupy one
of the most influential positions in American church
life. Before the war of 1939 it had become the fashion
to sneer at freedom as it operated in capitalist democ-
racies. This was a Marxist achievement. "Bourgeois
freedom" was a hollow sham, and so on. But bitter
experience has taught us a sobering lesson. We know
today that even "capitalist freedom" is precious, and
much to be preferred to the slavery which has been
clamped down on culture and politics in Germany and
Russia. It was a great thing that, in Niebuhr's case, the
men who chiefly paid the piper did *not* call the tune.
The tune played by Niebuhr was a fundamental criticism of the accepted ideology and tradition. By the
written and the spoken word, he trained a constant
battery of fire on the hallowed assumptions and values
of American Christianity. But not only of American
Christianity.

No single thinker has done more than Niebuhr to reveal the bankruptcy of secular illusions and ideals in our time. If it is true, as Professor Grant says, that "all revolutions begin in the minds of men," then Niebuhr is in the front rank of contemporary revolutionaries, Christian or secular. By his acute and profound analysis of events and institutions, by his bold and powerful application of Christian theological orthodoxy to secular processes and affairs, Niebuhr has done a great deal to undermine confidence in secular ideas and ideals. For thirty years he has poured forth a steady stream of illuminating social criticism from pulpit and professorial chair; by books which have been read throughout two continents; and by weighty and solid periodical journalism. The importance of all this work cannot be measured and certainly cannot be over-estimated. One evidence of its value is that Niebuhr is the Christian theologian most quoted by secular sociologists and publicists both in the United States and Great Britain today. Niebuhr has done all this work, not as a bookish recluse, but as a practical man immersed in daily contacts with average humanity. His movement to the left has shaken loose American Christianity from its attachment to the right. He is a standing witness to the power of the individual in a world that is being strangled by organization.

4

The Christian Revolutionary in Being

Having at one time been saturated by Hegelian dialectic, first in its pure form and later in its inverted Marxist form, I confess that I find it difficult to disengage my mind completely from dialectic. The penalty of this baptism by total immersion is that one tends to see dialectic where possibly it doesn't exist. Perhaps, therefore, it is somewhat fanciful—or more than somewhat, as Niebuhr's fellow countryman, Damon Runyon, would say—to see the ubiquitous curse of dialectic in the development of Reinhold Niebuhr. Let the reader then treat this as a bit of light relief. In Niebuhr's movement to the right, behold the *thesis*. In his movement to the left, behold the *antithesis*. And in the Christian revolutionary in being—there is the synthesis! Right-wing theology and left-wing politics, having duly interpenetrated each other, merge into the grand negation of the negation to achieve a positive balanced person. But this presentation of Niebuhr is not all nonsense, though a great deal of it most certainly is.

Niebuhr is a theologian. It is most necessary to insist on this point, because it has a most important bearing on any evaluation of Niebuhr's place and significance. He is a theologian—but a theologian with a difference.

73

He is a "throw-back"—I dare not use the word "re-actionary"—to the medieval Catholic and early Refor-mation tradition of theology. In modern, post-reforma-tion theology, the word "theologian" has shrunk into a narrower connotation. It has come to mean one whose materials of thought are ecclesiastical experiences, re-ligious experience in the specific sense of a reference of thought, will and feeling, separate from the rest of life. The word has come to connote one who is concerned with the intellectual presentation of a field of experience separate from the rest of life, as an artist pursuing a specialist activity. Now in an earlier tradition theology was regarded as the religious aspect of the whole of life. This was the character which Aquinas, for in-stance, bore as a theologian. He examined the religious aspect of what we today think of as purely secular activity. But in Aquinas's day theology was "the queen of the sciences," and therefore laid all the sciences un-der toll. The reformers were in the same tradition, more aggressively, which means that the tradition of treating theology as the religious aspect of universal experience was beginning to disintegrate. Political activity and theorizing was as familiar an element in Reformation theology as mystical, religious experience in the nar-rower sense of the word.

It is this tradition which Niebuhr has done so much to recover, to the undoubted advantage of theological thinking today. He combines religious thought *per se* with secular sociological thought. His work is a genu-ine synthesis of the two, and in so doing he has greatly deepened the whole concept of revolution. He has uncovered a deeper dimension in revolutionary thought and activity. He shows that, beneath the political surface of the revolutionary process, there is a moral theological activity. Revolution, which is an affair of men, is still more an affair of divine Providence. To put the same thing in another way, Niebuhr's work as a theologian is concerned largely with the religious implications of economic, political and social theory and practice. One of the first things that impressed me about him was that here was a theologian who, obviously, had a thorough knowledge of revolutionary, political theory, a combination which to me at that time was a striking novelty. Equipped as he was with the usual religious study, in the narrower sense of the term, he was additionally equipped with a thorough knowledge of secular sociology.

This is the synthesis which Niebuhr has achieved between professional religious knowledge and secular sociological theory. It is this which constituted his fine equipment as a Christian revolutionary. It is this, too, which endows him with so much authority and significance in an age of social disintegration. It is this that marks him as a mature Christian revolutionary in being.

Niebuhr is not only a theorist. Like Marx, he combines theory with practice, but, unlike Marx, he does not arrogate the sole right to judge what is correct practice. Marx founded the First International, and finally wrecked it. One of Niebuhr's most considerable achievements as a Christian revolutionary was the part he played in founding, not an international, but an inter-church Fellowship of Socialist Christians, which has continued to grow steadily. In addition to works of practical support of social causes, as opportunity offers from time to time,[1] it conducts a thorough-going Christian propaganda of social interpretation in the pages of its quarterly journal, *Christianity and Society* (which originally bore the title *Radical Religion*).

The amount of writing Niebuhr does in this journal incidentally illustrates his tremendous energy and vitality. In every issue he writes the commentary on events as well as many of the reviews, which reveal that he has read the books he reviews. It is the commentary, however, which discloses the Christian revolutionary in full being. There is nothing else in contemporary Christian journalism quite equal to it—or, for that matter, in secular journalism either. Mr. Douglas Woodruff, in the Roman Catholic *Tablet,* comes nearest—which is frequently very near. It is criticism, theological, profound and prophetic. I present a few examples, which illustrate Niebuhr's power of extracting the permanent issue from the passing event.

In 1938, Karl Barth wrote a letter to a Czech soldier in which he stated that by waging war against Hitler he would be defending the liberty of the Church as well as the security of his own country. Here is Niebuhr's comment:

---

[1] Here are a few examples: the raising of a special fund to help in the rescue of anti-nazis in Europe; regular support of refugees from nazism in Europe; regular conferences on special problems of labour; investigation of special distress among lower-paid workers; study of relations in America between the Negroes and whites.

"We find these judgments astonishing, though we agree with them politically. They are astonishing because they come from a man who has spent all his energies to prove that it is impossible to mix relative political judgments with the unconditioned demands of the Gospel. Nothing discredits Barth's major theological emphasis more than his complete abandonment of his primary thesis in the hour of crisis. . . . We agree neither with Barth's previous separation of the Gospel from fateful political and historical decisions which we as men must make, nor yet with his present identification of the Czech soldier with the liberty of the Church of Christ. Surely Barth ought to be the last man to believe that the Church will be wiped out if the Hitlers and Mussolinis are not defeated. It may be forced into the catacombs, but the more the ridiculous Caesar-gods rage the more apparent it will become that Christianity is true and that it is the ultimate truth. The majesty of God is most perfectly revealed in the movement when the Christ is crucified. The gates of hell cannot prevail against this Church. . . . On the other hand it is quite true that the fate of a Christian civilization may well be decided or could have been decided by Czech soldiers. There is a difference between a civilization which seeks to build itself on the Gospel foundations and one which explicitly defies the Gospel. This difference is tremendous and it is worth fighting for. . . . A culture lives in a civilization, and a civilization is a physical thing which can be destroyed and can be saved. But a culture is nothing more than a rationalization of a civilization if it is not also the fruit of a religion which is not primarily concerned about the future of cultures and civilizations" (*Radical Religion,* Vol. IV, no. 1, pp. 4–5).

Here is Niebuhr's interpretation of the German-Soviet pact of August, 1939:

"What does strike one with horror is the communist defence of this procedure; the desperate effort which is being made to keep Russia clad in the shining armour of righteousness. The communist papers tell us that Stalin circumvented the Chamberlain policy of appeasement, that the fear of the great Red Army brought Hitler to heel, that Stalin broke the Axis by dissociating Japan from Germany, etc. This is to make black white and white black in a fashion reminiscent of nazi propaganda. The arguments outrage the simplest logic. A pact which sets Germany free to fight does not circumvent appeasement. It is appeasement on a larger scale than ever attempted by Chamberlain. . . . What appals us particularly is the spiritual poverty which forces so many people in our era to talk this nonsense in order to save themselves from despair. One must continue to defend and to extend if possible whatever decency, justice and freedom still exist in this day when the lights are going out one by one. One can do that with clearest vision and courage if one has not placed one's faith in some frail reed of human virtue which does not exist. It is well for all Christians who have not fled into

quietism but who have a sense of responsibility toward the problem of civilization to recognize clearly
that the tragedy of our era is not merely the decay
of a capitalistic-bourgeois social order; but the corruption of its alternative socialist order almost as
soon as it had established itself. This does not mean
that the task of advancing democracy to include economic justice as well as political justice is a hopeless
one. After all, bourgeois democracy did succeed in
destroying feudalism, despite Napoleon's treason
and, one might add, despite the degeneration of
Cromwell's city of God into the first tyranny of
modern history. The Kingdom of God is not of this
world; yet its light illumines our tasks in this world
and its hope saves us from despair. The Christian
faith stands between the illusions and the despair of
the world; it is particularly an antidote to the illusions which are stubbornly held in defiance of the
facts in order to save men from despair" (*op. cit.,*
Vol. IV, no. 4, pp. 2–3).

These two examples show the quality of Niebuhr's
work in social criticism and interpretation. He discloses
the moral and spiritual issues involved in the outer
event. Nothing that he has done exceeds in importance
this which I do not hesitate to call "contemporary
prophesying." It reveals history as the arena of a divine
Providence.

*   *   *

Turning from the practical activities of Niebuhr to
his character as a Christian revolutionary, let us seek

to understand the distinctive principles which determined his prophetic inspiration and outlook. In other
words, what are the elements into which his long
struggle for clarity and coherence in Christian faith has
finally crystallized, which inspire his revolutionary
Christian consciousness? What are the lights by which
"the revolutionary in being" steers his course in a complex world? I think they can be reduced to four.

*First is the principle of the relevance of an absolute,
transcendent gospel to a relative situation; the applica-
bility of Christianity to every social situation.*

Now this principle is not so simple as it seems. It is
in fact one of the profoundest significance. As we have
seen, one of Niebuhr's earliest discoveries was the im-
possibility of a direct simple application of Christian
ethic to the actual historic situation. This realization
penetrates all his thinking and all his writing. No theme
recurs as frequently as this in his work. It is the ground
on which he chiefly criticizes liberal Christianity and
pacifism. Niebuhr denies that the Kingdom of God is
a historic possibility at all. You cannot apply what are
called the principles of the Sermon on the Mount to
sinful nations and societies in this world any more than
you can play Beethoven's "Hammerklavier" on a side-
board. The illusion that you can, Niebuhr sees to be
the greatest weakness in pacifism. The sum total of
Christian ethic is contained in the injunction to love
our neighbors as ourselves, the so-called "law of love."
The pacifist assumes that this is a social possibility.
But, says Niebuhr, it is not. It is a delusive simplification of a vast complexity. It is also a radical confusion

and misunderstanding of the Christian gospel, including its "law of love," which is not a "law" at all. Christianity is not a revision of Jewish legalism. "The significance of the law of love is precisely that it is not just another law, but a law which transcends all law." Niebuhr will have no truck with the assumption that the law of love can be made an operative principle in political and social relationships.

Now the simple, obvious conclusion to be drawn from this would seem to be that Christianity is not applicable at all to society, that the Christian faith has no relevance to history. The fact that Niebuhr did not draw this conclusion is profoundly significant. The obvious conclusion was a false conclusion, which suggests that the obvious and the true do not always coincide. But this was the conclusion which Lutheranism, in which Niebuhr was reared, tended to draw. To say that Luther himself drew this conclusion, that he handed the state over to the Devil, is much too unqualified a statement. But there was sufficient in Lutheranism to lend color to this idea, as is proved by the fact that that tendency had crystallized into pietism in Germany by the eighteenth century. The denial of all relevance of Christianity to the historic situation, however, was much too simple. It was in fact a mere inversion of Christian liberalism. In the undue simplification of Christianity, the extremes of pacifism and, shall we say, Bismarckism meet. Niebuhr, though he denied the possibility of a simple application of Christian ethic, did not embrace the opposite error of denying all application. The Christian faith still has rele-

vance to history. As we have seen, Niebuhr criticized
Barth for his too absolute denial of this very point.

Now without attempting exhaustive discussion of
what Niebuhr conceives to be the nature of the Christian relevance to society,[2] it may be stated that its essence lies in two directions: as an abiding judgment of
human pride and sin; and as a dynamic approximation
to perfect justice. The significance of these two state-
ments will perhaps be better appreciated if we understand first of all what Niebuhr means by the Gospel.

"The good news of the Gospel is not the law that we
ought to love one another. The good news of the
Gospel is that there is a resource of divine mercy
which is able to overcome a contradiction within our
souls, which we cannot ourselves overcome. The
contradiction is that, though we know we ought to
love our neighbor as ourself, there is a law in our
members which wars against the law in our minds.
So that, in fact, we love ourselves more than our
neighbor. The grace of God which is revealed in
Christ is regarded by Christian faith as, on the one
hand, an actual 'power of righteousness' which heals
the contradiction within our hearts. In that sense
Christ defines the actual possibilities of human existence. On the other hand, this grace is conceived

---

[2] The reader is referred to *An Interpretation of Christian Ethics*
for his discussion of this problem, especially to chapters iv, v and
vi. The idea that Christianity still is relevant when its ethics is not
applicable is so great a violation of conventional assumptions that
the reader may find it difficult to comprehend. Persistent study of
Niebuhr will reward the seeker on this point.

as 'justification,' as pardon rather than power, as
the forgiveness of God, which is vouchsafed to man
despite the fact that he never achieves the full measure of Christ. In that sense Christ is 'the impossible
possibility.' Loyalty to him means realization in in-
tention, but does not actually mean the full realization of the measure of Christ. In this doctrine of
forgiveness and justification, Christianity measures
the full seriousness of sin as a permanent factor in
human history. Naturally the doctrine has no meaning for a secular civilization, nor for the secularized
and moralized versions of Christianity. They cannot understand the doctrine precisely because they
believe there is some fairly simple way out of the
sinfulness of human history" (*Christianity and
Power Politics*, pp. 2–3).

What Niebuhr calls here "a contradiction in our
souls" is a complex of two things, that in fact man
never satisfies the ideal, but nevertheless believes that
he can. But the belief is an illusion. Man never will
satisfy the ideal. The illusion that he will is a protection
for his pride, which, once broken—radically broken—
would reduce man to despair. So all history, civilization
and culture are a conspiracy to defend man's pride,
which they effect by the renewal of illusion. Now Christianity as judgment is precisely to bring man to despair,
which is reality, to the acknowledgment of his utter inability ever to fulfill the ideal. But in the realization of
that very despair lies man's great hope; for in the
realization of despair judgment becomes mercy. Des-

pair becomes the venue of a rebirth of the whole man. And this is the profundity of the relevance of Christian faith to every historical situation. It is to deprive man of his pride, which dooms civilization to perpetual frustration. Christianity as judgment is the point of a new leverage in historical development.

By insisting then upon the relevance of the Gospel to the whole of life, Niebuhr is enabled to extract from every situation its maximum contribution to the moral well-being of society and the individual.

* * *

The second principle is that the historic process is envisaged always in terms of person. Niebuhr's revolutionism is for the release of personality.

The abiding sin of reformers and revolutionaries is the tendency to "black-out" the individual. And it always happens to a greater or less degree, generally greater. In the totalitarian socialisms of today, this tendency becomes practically absolute. In the national-socialism of Germany and the Soviet socialism of Russia the individual counts for next to nothing. It is the objective process that matters. This is the final logic of something inevitable in the revolutionary temper, though it is not inevitable that it should achieve its final logic. Once we become involved in "movements" we imperceptibly begin to think of the historical results of our activities as things somehow divorced from people, from individuals of flesh and blood, who laugh and cry, eat and drink and sleep, suffer and rejoice. It is the supreme sin of all revolutionary movements. Opponents

are, of course, absolutely divested of personality. They
are objectified, categorized, depersonalized. They are
"they"—capitalist class, *ancien régime,* the exploiters
or what-not. They cease to be thought of as human. If
revolutions teach anything at all, they surely demon-
strate that the dehumanization of opponents inevitably
leads to the dehumanization of allies and supporters too.
That is why the great historic revolutions always de-
vour their own children—none more so than the most
recent of the series, the Russian revolution.

The source of this is the divorce in our vision between process and person. The process becomes a thing-
in-itself, a vested interest, for the defense of which individuals come to be regarded as instruments. Revolutions, alas!, are a necessity in a world of irrational
humanity. But they breed a temper more vicious, cruel
and callous than that which wars breed. Witness the
disturbances in liberated Greece: the Greek factions
hated one another more than they did the Germans. I
experienced the same thing directly in Spain during the
civil war: anarchist and communist hated each other
far more than either hated Franco. The individual
vanished as a person. He is transformed into a mere
element in a process, from whence proceeds a tragic
result; the aims of revolution are lost in the whirlpool
of power, and the struggle to maintain it.

Niebuhr thinks fundamentally in terms of the person. Not only does he think in terms of the person, he
also feels in the same terms. That is to say, in this matter of historic process and personality, his thought and
emotion are integrated. Niebuhr would be the last man

in the world to claim that he is immune from the poison
of power. But it makes all the difference in the world
in revolutionary action and procedure whether the exercise of power has to contend with settled convictions
which can check and delimit the inevitable abuse of
power. This is precisely the social and political significance of personalism, of the envisaging of process as
an affair of living men and women. The same truth can
be put in another way. The secular revolutionary loves
mankind, humanity. The Christian revolutionary loves
men, individuals. The significance of this distinction
cannot be exaggerated for politics and social action.
Love for mankind can be combined with hatred for the
individual, which is one of the most appalling characteristics of revolutionary fervor in European history.
One thinks, for instance, of the father of that tortured
individual, Mirabeau. He was known as "Friend of the
People"; but his treatment of his son was cold and
cruel. It is fatally easy to love man in the mass, because
no attitude lends itself more conveniently to the camou-
flaging and rationalization of self-love and will-to-
power than a passionate love for man in the mass. Like
every other human activity, love for man as person
lends itself also to the corrupting element of sin and
pride—but with more difficulty, since the relationship is
direct. Self-deception has less room in which to hide in
a direct personal relationship than in remote institutional relationships. This goes back to Niebuhr's days
in Detroit. As we have already learnt, the social problem presented itself to him then in the shape of concrete individuals, whose problems, anxieties and condi-

tions were his personal care. That habit or attitude he has carried with him to this very day. It has shaped and molded his whole social theory. And not only his social theory. The profound Christian character of his sociology determines his view of the entire historic process as one of ultimate personal release. In the last analysis, Niebuhr's vision of human fulfillment is not Utopia, but the Communion of Saints, which admirably defines the difference between men as a mass and man as a person.

* * *

The third directive principle is awareness of the operation in oneself of the element of corruption which is seen to be operating in the whole historic process. Theologically expressed, the prophet himself also stands under the judgment which he pronounces upon society.

Here again, this is a principle (or achievement) which looks much simpler than it really is. The proof of the depth and complexity of this principle is the fact of the rarity of its realization. How many preachers, for instance, are aware of the extent to which they are involved in the sins they so confidently condemn? The confidence of their condemnation is a demonstration of their unconsciousness. True prophecy is not a mere pronouncement, but a burdened utterance, for it tells of a doom which involves the prophet himself. Careless rapture may be the experience of the artist and poet. But the prophet is not an artist: he is an oracle. How many revolutionaries (to take another example) are there who are conscious of the degree to which they participate in the very exploitation which they professedly abhor—or, which is much less, are aware of the mere fact that they do participate to even the slightest degree?

As has already been argued, revolution particularly breeds self-righteousness, and revolutionaries generally see themselves as "innocent of the great transgression." The factional struggle for power in Russia after the death of Lenin exemplifies cruelly this moral and spiritual unconsciousness. And this unawareness of self-corruption in the bolshevik revolutionaries was appallingly costly in human lives. The world, in all probability, will never have the opportunity to study the statistics of the gigantic butcheries of the Stalin-Trotsky conflict. We can see the operation of the same sin in the wider arena of international strife. The victor's delusion that he is innocent altogether has nearly always been the seed of a new fatal political development. This does not mean, for example, that we should make no distinction between nazi crimes of policy and Allied policy. Doffing the white sheet of innocence does not mean that we should don the black sheet of the enemy. This is where so many pacifists violate the most elementary moral realities. There is a vast relative difference between what the nazis have done and even the worst things that the Allies have done. But Europe will more quickly recover health and sanity if the victors show some awareness that they too have had some responsibility for the sin of nazism.

This simple-seeming principle, then, has profound, far-reaching and incalculable consequences for society.

It can make a difference of life and death for millions of human beings. It can make a difference between intolerable misery and suffering and quiet happiness for still greater millions of ordinary human beings, who ask for nothing more than the right to pursue their own way of life, to enjoy the intimate delight and to suffer the petty irritations of daily family routine. And it can make the difference of progress and decay for whole civilizations. We too readily assume that simply because certain events did happen that they were bound to happen, that nothing different could have happened, which does not follow. Given the domination of the character of statesman and revolutionary by pride, by *hubris,* the congruent event is almost inevitable. But the unchecked sway of pride is not inevitable. For instance, it is not unreasonable to assume that, had the First International been guided by Engels instead of Marx, its history would have been different. The whole point of Christianity in relation to personal character is that the miracle of change is always a real possibility. Simultaneous change in all the actors of a particular social situation is not a historic possibility, with the result that the application of the maximum wisdom in any given situation is not a possibility either. But sufficient change to modify a situation is a historic possibilty.

Not the least of the many contributions which Niebuhr has made both to theology and sociology has been his demonstration of the implications for politics of Christian virtues. When these are made plain in the way Niebuhr has shown, then they seem obvious and platitudinous. But that is always the case. Nobody has quite revealed the profound political implications of simple Christian humility as Niebuhr has done; it looks ordinary when demonstrated. But what a difference to society a practical demonstration would make is sufficiently suggested by the example of Niebuhr himself. His realization that the corruption which he sees in action in the things and people he criticizes is operating also in himself makes of him a rare kind of revolutionary. It makes a revolutionary who is not only emancipated from illusions about the decaying order, but also unburdened by illusions about the emerging order.

* * *

The fourth of the principles defining the equipment of "the revolutionary in being" is that comprehension and balance are the result of appreciation of the truth in both sides of the conflict; in the appropriation of the permanent values both of tradition and of progress, of the old and the new.

Niebuhr is, in other words, a true "dialectician." It is this quality in him which makes his writing difficult to so many people. But a little reflection should show that, in the dialectical character of his thinking and writing, Niebuhr reduces to self-conscious science what is confused and unconscious in the unthinking mind. Nobody in fact lives and thinks in terms only of the moment. Such a process is inconceivable. We all of us, the untrained and the most highly trained, unconsciously relate the past to the present. We carry and preserve much of the old in our appropriation of the new. We do not start every day *de novo*. We perpetuate something of the past in all our thinking. Dialectical thinking is a refinement and a complication of that habit and process.

Now if, as Hegel maintains, the *synthesis* is an integration, a weaving into one, of the abiding elements in the *thesis* and the *antithesis,* then nothing can be more undialectical than to think of the old, the traditional, the passing order, in terms of destruction only. This is, in fact, the style and accent of so much Marxist propaganda, in which capitalism, for example, has become wholly evil. This is the great defect of secular utopian thinking. Change has become a good in itself. Change for change's sake, in short. This too is what makes the secular left such a menace to civilization. It leads to a depreciation of tradition, which G. K. Chesterton called "the democracy of the dead." Tradition must be a contemporary factor if civilization is to remain healthy and secure. The votes of the dead should at least be weighed. But utopian, progressive secularism tends to see good only in the future, which means, in fact, that it never sees any good at all; for the future never comes. In the moment of becoming it ceases to be future. It becomes only the drab present bereft of the good which was envisaged yesterday.

Now Niebuhr sees the vitality of tradition as well as the dynamic of progress, the future against the background of the past. The most obvious example of this in his case is his apparently paradoxical balancing of traditional (orthodox) theology and progressive politics—"right in theology and left in politics."

This effective dialectical habit has made possible for

Niebuhr the rare achievement of being able to retain the gains, the insights, which he has won from ideas and a mode of thinking since discarded; he carries them forward into new attitudes, when the old are transcended. He treasures the substance though the form disappears. Most thinkers lose the insights which came to them through ideas since abandoned. The essence of an idea, belief, creed or attitude can only be apprehended and appropriated from the inside. One can only feel or see the essence of toryism, for instance, by being a tory really and truly. Niebuhr has never been a tory: but he has been many things which he is no longer, and the insight gained from those abandoned philosophies he still retains. In the last war he was a pacifist, and if the reader makes a study of his booklet, *Why the Christian Church Is Not Pacifist,* he will see an example of Niebuhr's perpetuated insight. This is why his thought is so rich and comprehensive.

This principle it is which makes of Niebuhr the rarest of all kinds of revolutionaries—the balanced revolutionary. Revolutionaries are necessarily extremists. Most of them are singular extremists—*i.e.,* obsessed with one idea or attitude. Niebuhr is also an extremist, but a plural extremist. He is obsessed with opposing extremes, whose tension makes for balance. And this is the true Christian revolutionary attitude. He keeps in tension time and eternity, which meet in man. This is what makes for Christian dynamic. G. K. Chesterton has described the paradox of Christian virtue and character in *Orthodoxy,* where he says that the truly Christian man practices opposite virtues to extravagance. To preserve in relation opposing elements, as Niebuhr does, makes for width as well as depth. It also makes for tolerance and charity. Niebuhr nourishes the old through its integration into the new.

Here then we see the revolutionary in being—responsible, human and humane; humble and burdened, and balanced and comprehensive. It is a formidable combination of qualities. It helps to explain his increasing influence on thoughtful people in two continents.

5

"The Theory of the Permanent Revolution"

I HAVE borrowed the title of this section from Trotsky's book of the same name. In a very much profounder way, Niebuhr's view of Christianity commits the Church, as the historic agent and vehicle of the Gospel, to a "theory of permanent revolution" in the literal sense. It commits the Church to a fundamental opposition to the world till the very end of time. Trotsky's permanent revolution was only pseudo-permanent, because he envisaged its fulfillment within history—indeed within the contemporary phase of history. But Niebuhr's revolution is synchronous with the whole of the time-process—and beyond. If the Church is to be faithful to her Lord and his Gospel, she must wage war against the world for the entire duration of history, until it is swallowed up in the eternal order. This is permanent revolution indeed.

Sufficient has been said in preceding pages to indicate Niebuhr's conviction that the Kingdom of God is not a possibility for history. His whole outlook is so saturated with this conviction that it can be said, without the least exaggeration, that it comes out in every other sentence of his written work. This conviction has probably been the source of the most prolific misunder-

standing of Niebuhr's teaching. This misunderstanding
has been so crass, in some cases, as to accuse him of
being an escapist from history—a thing against which
he is constantly at war. Whatever charge can be leveled
against Niebuhr, one thing of which he cannot possibly
be justly accused is of running away from the attempt
to deal christianly with the historic situation. The application of the Gospel to history and the real manner in
which that may be done is the connecting theme of all
his work and it can be illustrated by a remark of Dr.
Orchard's. Castigating the too-easy American attitude
to divorce, "In some of the American states," said
Orchard, "divorce can be obtained on the ground of
'incompatibility of temperament.' Why! *that is the object of marriage!*" So it may be said of Niebuhr, that
the object of all his thinking is to discover how the
Gospel can be applied to civilization. His denial that the
Kingdom of God is a historic possibility is for the purpose of clearing the ground of illusions and misconcep-
tions, so as to discover how it can really and truly be
applied.

This ludicrous misinterpretation of Niebuhr arises,
as suggested in my preface, from a too innocent un-
familiarity with the dialectical character of his thinking. Men trained, as we nearly all have been trained,
in the tradition of a too formal logic, with its simple
"either . . . or" find it difficult to adapt themselves to
the more complex processes of a more realistic logic
with its "both . . . and." Niebuhr is painfully aware
of the deeper complexity of existence, which is missed
by the clearer rationalist. His richer perceptions are

partly due to his realization of the fact of original sin. "The truth is," writes Niebuhr, "that, absurd as the classical Pauline doctrine of original sin may seem to be at first blush, its prestige as a part of the Christian truth is preserved, and perennially re-established, against the attacks of rationalists and moralists by its ability to throw light upon complex factors in human behavior which constantly escape the moralists." Inability to perceive the tragic contradictions of human nature strengthens the attachment of the simple rationalist and the still simpler moralist to the inadequate ratiocinative processes of formal logic. A doctrine of logic which makes inconsistency in thinking the greatest intellectual sin incapacitates men from appreciation of concrete, objective inconsistencies of act and will which do in fact exist. That is what history is—a complex of contradictory acts, policies and institutions.

It may be well, therefore, to say that, though Niebuhr denies the possibility of historic realization of the divine Kingdom, he strenuously insists that the Kingdom is, nevertheless, operative in history.

"It is important to recognize that the Kingdom of God, according to the biblical conception, is never purely an other-worldly perfection, not even when it is interpreted in a gospel which is directed primarily to the Greek world. The Christian is taught to pray constantly 'Thy Kingdom come.' The hope of this prayer, when vital, is a constant pressure upon the conscience of man in every action. The kingdom which is not of this world is in this world, through

man and in man, who is in this world, and yet not altogether of this world. Man is not of this world in
the sense that he can never rest complacently in the
sinful standards which are normative in this world.
He may be selfish but he cannot accept selfishness as
the standard of conduct. He may be greedy but he
knows that greed is wrong. Even when his actions
do not conform to his ideals he cannot dismiss his
ideals as irrelevant. . . . The kingdom which is not
of this world is always in this world in man's uneasy
conscience." [1]

* * *

The permanent revolution is thus involved, not only
in the conflict between the relative achievements of
history and the absolute ideal, but also in the character
and structure of human nature, which is itself a tension
of two worlds, two orders of being. Man is a two-
dimensional entity, and cannot therefore escape the fate
of an unresolved contradiction in the present time-
order. But does not the theory of a permanent revolution involve a theory of organization for conducting it?
In other words, the theory of a church? It is in trying
to answer this question that there is ground for a legitimate and much more serious criticism of Niebuhr.

In any realist discussion of the problem of the relation between Church and World, of the distinction and

---

[1] *Beyond Tragedy*, pp. 278-9. The reader should ponder the whole
chapter from which the above passage is quoted. It is an address
entitled "The Kingdom Not of This World." It is an excellent example—and one of the less difficult ones—of Niebuhr's way of
thinking.

opposition between them, the question of the nature of
the Church *as an organized body* is fundamental and
inescapable. If the Gospel is first of all, as Niebuhr
says, a proclamation of the mercy and judgment of
God, if the redemption of mankind is wholly the work
of God, it is clear that without a body committed
wholly to that proclamation it cannot be historically
operative and effective. In other words, the historic witness to the Gospel necessitates a church; for without
a church the Gospel would be lost in human disintegration and corruption. Without a church, in other words,
the Christian revolution loses its permanence. The
Gospel would be corrupted into identification with the
current, conventional moralities. The Church alone has
preserved the Gospel as a transcendent distinctive
reality in the world. Whenever, for instance, the
formulation of doctrine has threatened the distinctive-
ness of the Gospel as Redemption, as in the Arian con-
troversy, it was the Church that saved the situation.
Whenever, again, the Church has threatened to become wholly ineffective as the historic guardian of the
Gospel, as in the era of the Reformation, it is the Holy
Spirit within the Church—not diffused through society, but within the sacramental body of the Church—
that has re-fashioned the Church to its essential mission. The discussion, therefore, of the Church as a
historic, organized entity, is not a mere ecclesiastical
luxury. It is fundamental *to the Gospel*.

It is on this question that Niebuhr is theologically
defective. His neglect of this whole field of theology
does afford legitimate ground for criticism. His ab-

sorption in the various issues of the Gospel as an independent proclamation, as an entity in itself, in its transcendental aspect divorced from its historic community with the Church, has resulted in a neglect of a fundamentally significant field of theology. It has been said justly, for instance, that Niebuhr is very "cavalier in his attitude to the question of ministerial order." [2] This is symbolical of a radical defect in Niebuhr's outlook. Perhaps, deep down, this is what Canon Raven and others feel and mean when they say that Niebuhr is "not a theologian." It is his unawareness of the importance of all those questions which in the narrower sense are conceived within the Church in her relation to herself, so to speak. He has concentrated, to an undialectical extent, on the problem of the relation of the Gospel to *civilization* to the almost complete neglect of its relation to *the Church*. I give one example of this.

What is the significance and value of episcopacy in the economy of the Church? As far as I know, Niebuhr has nowhere raised or explored this question, which is vital to the existence of the Church, and therefore to the whole problem of the relation between Christianity and civilization.[3] Whatever else may be charged against him, the one thing he cannot be accused of is indifference to

---

[2] By the Rev. A. R. Vidler, who is excelled by nobody in appreciation of Niebuhr.

[3] Here we must write with some reserve. I am familiar with everything which Niebuhr has published in book form and also with a great deal of his journalism. It is possible, of course, that he has written on questions of church organization etc., and that these writings have escaped me—which I doubt. None of them are in book form. Neither has any hint of these questions come out in personal discussions.

the problem of the relation of Christianity to civilization. Yet the effectiveness of the Gospel as a historic
power depends on a question which has very little place
in Niebuhr's thinking, in so far as his thinking is evi-
denced by his published work. Is episcopacy of divine
ordination, which is the Catholic (not simply Roman)
contention? Is it a necessity of church constitution?
Can the Church continue to function effectively without
it? From this question arises a whole range of cognate
questions—what constitutes ordination, ministerial authority, the place of the sacraments? These questions—
every one of them—are not merely ecclesiastical, but
are, finally, of profound sociological significance. Just
as Lenin's theory of party constitution has been vital
for the development of the Russian revolution, which,
in its turn, has been of enormous significance for
Europe and the world (and is going to prove of still
greater significance in the post-war world), so this
question of episcopacy and cognate issues is ultimately
vital for civilization, as well as for the Church. The
theory of the permanent revolution—the Christian revolution—is tied up with it. It is therefore not too much
to argue that Niebuhr's neglect of this field of theology
is a serious inadequacy, both for a theologian and for
a Christian revolutionary.

The inevitable tendency of Niebuhr's work, however,
is toward the sharpening of the issue of Church versus
World. No contemporary theologian has done more to
define that issue in current terms. The net result of his
work is to compel us, even the secularists amongst us,
to essay a reconsideration of the place and significance

of the Church as an historic institution, responsible
for the safe-keeping of the Gospel and its eternally
valid message. To the criticism which I have made here
of the balance of his work, Niebuhr may well reply
that no man can possibly cover the whole field of Christian theology. And that, of course, is true. But this
does not altogether meet the point, which is that what
is true and valid in one's own thinking inevitably suf-
fers some distortion when it is not balanced by its
complement. The necessary balancing problem of the
Gospel in relation to civilization is the Gospel in relation
to the Church. The tenor of Niebuhr's work is, in fact,
to focus that issue more decisively. And for this, every
thinking Christian man—which does not, unhappily,
mean every Christian man—will be duly grateful. In
this as in every other aspect of Christian thought and
practice, Niebuhr is always, in the finish, "on the side
of the angels."

* * *

Reinhold Niebuhr is a gift of God to a tortured and
troubled world. He is, by any standard of judgment
whatsoever, a leading, if not the leading, theorist in the
contemporary revolution in Christian thought. He has
made orthodox theology relevant to our secular crisis.
He has made it intellectually respectable. In our optimistic youth, many of us drifted into liberal Protestant-
ism because we shared too easily the assumption that
orthodoxy was intellectually discredited. It had ceased
to be fashionable. It was out of date. Every bright
young thing was modernist by definition. Niebuhr has

powerfully helped to change all that. Nowadays, it is the old who are theological liberals. The young, who as always tend to swim with the tide, are orthodox. Niebuhr has been one of the influences that have reversed the theological tide. But he has done more than that. By his prophetic insight and passion, he has made the Christian faith an inescapable social issue for a generation whose own secular faith has proved to be bankrupt. This achievement makes his place secure in the apostolical succession of Christian revolutionaries.